The Education Act 1870

The Education Act 1870

A study of public opinion

Eric E. Rich, M.A. (Cantab), Ph.D. (Lond)

LONGMANS

LONGMANS, GREEN AND CO LTD
London and Harlow

*Associated companies, branches and representatives
throughout the world*

© Longmans, Green and Co Ltd 1970
First published 1970

SBN 582 32490 4

*Printed in U.K. by
Spottiswoode, Ballantyne & Co Ltd
London and Colchester*

Contents

Foreword

Dr Eric Rich has written a highly interesting book on public opinion and the Education Act of 1870, which I have greatly enjoyed reading. He gives a full and admirable account of the detailed provisions of the Act; but the value of the book lies most of all in the skill with which Dr Rich relates the history of the passage of the Act to the educational, social, political and economic beliefs that were most widely held in mid-Victorian England.

Dr Rich stresses in particular, the basic point that 'The Education Act was different from other legislation of the reformers of the nineteenth century. It did not merely provide for inspection to see that the law was obeyed. . . . It was a positive law which secured school accommodation for all children whose parents did not pay a school fee exceeding ninepence a week. . . [It] placed the State in a new relation to society.' It is easy, with hindsight, to forget what a courageous step this was. Dr Rich pertinently reminds us of the difficulties involved in granting substantial powers to School Boards, since 'local government was not trusted in the nineteenth century'. The issue of local rates as a source of educational finance was politically explosive; as Lord Salisbury, the future Prime Minister, was to say in debate: 'If in addition to the other burdens which land has to bear, you assume that it should also bear the expenses of national education, you will create a spirit of resistance which will secure for your system an amount of unpopularity which no improvement you may make in education will be able to counterbalance.' Lastly there was the immensely difficult 'Religious Conflict', as Dr Rich calls it: 'The state in most of its attempts to secure educational efficiency was opposed by one or other religious body. . . . The Church accepted educational grants, but was unwilling to concede any of its authority in return for them.' Actually, as Dr Rich shows, well over a thousand Voluntary Schools were transferred to School Boards before the end of the century; if only Church and State could have hit sooner on the device of the 'Voluntary Controlled School' (as very nearly happened after 1906), how much unnecessary discord might have been avoided.

Why, despite all these deterrents, did the Government decide to go ahead? Dr Rich's Chapter 6, which gives some of the reasons, is one of the most interesting in the book. He stresses the belief of so many contemporaries—a rather surprising one we may feel to-day

—that good secular education would prove an antidote to social and political unrest. Next, then as now, there were those who laid most emphasis on the importance of education as *investment*; as early as 1854 it was being said that 'Every day the special education of English workmen is becoming a commercial question of the deepest importance.' And Dr Rich does well to remind us that by 1867 'the industrial and the commercial competition of other countries was being keenly felt and the demand for industrial education increased'. In addition there were those Radicals who genuinely believed in educational advance for its own sake—who realised 'that education was something more than teaching the faith of our fathers, that the citizen of the nineteenth century was unfitted for social life without education, and that for each man to realise to some extent his capacities, he must be given the opportunities to develop them'. We may also add, I think, the influence of those in Parliament who were specially concerned with the problems of education as these affected particular areas. For instance, it was two highly influential Conservative M.P.s, Sandon and W. H. Smith, who persuaded Forster to set up a single School Board for the London Metropolis—a direct forerunner of the present-day Inner London Education Authority.

There are, of course, darker sides to Dr Rich's story. 'Education [in mid-Victorian England] was', he reminds us, 'associated with the idea of class distinction and the quality and quantity of education required for the children of one class was considered to be a separate problem from that required for those of another class of society.' In the unpleasantly frank words of the Taunton Commission 'The education of the gentry has gradually separated itself from that of the class below them and it is but natural that this class in their turn should be unwilling to be confounded with the labourers they employ.' We are reminded of that terrible episode in the contemporary school story *Eric or Little By Little* when the author, Dean Farrar, describes the ultimate degradation to which Eric on board ship was subjected: 'It was nobody's business to wait on him.'

But for the most part this is a story of promise and considerable achievement. Perhaps one set of figures, more than any other, tells its own tale: 'In England and Wales the number of certificated teachers rose from under 3,000 in 1855 to nearly 14,000 in 1870, to more than 62,000 in 1900, and to 129,000 by 1933.' The story of educational progress during the past hundred years is one of the most important chapters in the history of how, as a nation, we have come to a wider understanding of the true meaning of 'equal citizenship.'

EDWARD BOYLE

Introduction

This book does not attempt to follow in historical sequence the progress from one Education Bill to another until the Act of 1870 was passed; it is an attempt to study the interplay of ideas in the context of the educational institutions as they developed. Its roots are in lawmaking opinion, as Dicey expressed it, and such opinions are to be found in reports of parliamentary debates and in the institutions with which Members of Parliament were associated, though it has only been possible to sample a few of these.

Another source of law-making opinion is to be found in the reports of Her Majesty's Inspectors of Schools. These were men whose social standing was not inferior to that of the M.P.s themselves, and the views expressed in their reports and in their public utterances carried considerable weight. They were quoted in parliamentary debates, in the press, in the reports of the Newcastle Commission (1858–61) and Select Committees of the House of Commons. Their enthusiasm for the cause of education was of considerable importance.

So far as I have been able to discover there was no effective working-class opinion which influenced the development of law-making opinion. Many of the leading Chartists and Radicals were strongly in favour of a national system of education but it would be a mistake to think that they carried the working class with them; the earnings of the children were a strong counter argument which no amount of educational theory could outbalance.

The Act of 1870 was in itself a part of the law-making opinion of the years which followed, and, as befits a centenary volume, the last chapter gives some brief indication of its influence in the next hundred years. The hopes of 1870 have certainly flowered in a way that could not have been imagined by the politicians of the period.

Readers should note that where in the author's words 'dissenters' is spelt with a small 'd' it refers to all religious bodies other than the Church of England. With a capital 'D' it refers to the whole body of Nonconformists, that is those of Protestant faith who did not accept the Act of Uniformity of 1662.

The following abbreviations are used in the references: Hans. for Hansard's *Parliamentary Debates*; PP for Parliamentary Papers; and TNAPSS for *Transactions of the National Society for the Promotion of Social Science*.

This book is based on a thesis originally approved by the University of London for the Ph.D. (Econ.) degree and I would like to pay my tribute to the two supervisors of my studies the late Professor H. J. Laski and the late Professor R. H. Tawney who helped and encouraged me during the progress of the work. I also owe a debt to my wife, a debt which all married authors will recognise, and to my sister Miss K. Rich, B.A., whose workaday knowledge of the educational system from 1900 to 1945 has proved very useful.

Eric E. Rich

I

The Origins of the Idea of
State Education

Political, philosophical and religious ideas

The educational system of today, which is maintained by vast sums
from public funds, had small beginnings in the nineteenth century.
Indeed, there was at first considerable opposition to any government
aid for education, yet within seventy years the principle of state aid
was accepted. What explains this change in legislative opinion?

A. V. Dicey in his *Law and Public Opinion in England in the nineteenth
century* was the first to trace the development of law-making opinion,
and to his work (which is not perhaps sufficiently valued today) the
writer owes the idea which lies behind this volume. Dicey traces three
strands of thought in the opinion of this period; first the period of Old
Toryism to 1830; then the period of Benthamism to 1870; and finally
the period of Collectivism from 1865. By Old Toryism Dicey referred
to the main trend of legislative opinion which was opposed to any
marked change. This was in part due to the prevailing ideas of the
perfection of the constitution as taught by Blackstone, the celebrated
lawyer, and supported, in his own way, by the politician Edmund
Burke. There was also a conservative reaction against the ferment of
revolutionary politics on the continent. The excesses of the revolution
were deplored and the near perfection of British political institutions
was proved by the absence of revolution. The Tories of the period
were not averse to some legislation of a paternalistic kind, for they
were supporters of philanthropic causes, but any liberalising ideas
were anathema to them. The period of Benthamism Dicey identified
with ideas of individualism and *laissez-faire*, although he agreed that
laissez-faire did not necessarily follow from the utilitarian philosophy
of Bentham. As Professor Brebner has pointed out, Bentham himself
favoured legislative intervention to secure essential reforms, but
Bentham was also more than critical of the inefficient administration
of the state as it existed and he considered any extension of law and
government needed full justification because, fundamentally, they

were concerned with the restriction of liberty. Collectivist thought accepted the notion of the beneficial intervention of the state to achieve specific ends, though the end was not conceived of as socialism. Outside the sphere of social legislation the principle of *laissez-faire* was of general application. In the debates leading to the Education Act of 1870 all these strands of thought played an important part.

Tory philanthropy made a significant contribution, though wedded to the idea of religious education. The philanthropic legislation of the period, such as the Abolition of Slavery (1807 and 1833), the law of 1802 to improve the conditions of Poor Law apprentices in factories, the Factories Act of 1819, and even the lax administration of outdoor relief before 1834 all showed the influence of the benevolent paternalism of Tory ideas. But the tendency has been to place at too early a date the general influence of humanitarian ideals. The attention which has been concentrated on the slave trade, the legislative protection of pauper apprentices and the provision of better conditions for sailors has caused too much importance to be attached to these early movements. It should be remembered that the employment of children continued to increase after 1850 despite the growth of a feeling of kindness to animals. In 1833 there was a majority of five against Buckingham's motion in the House of Commons condemning the impressment of seamen in time of war. At a time when the Great Exhibition of 1851 was rousing public enthusiasm for the arts of peace, children of six and seven could be kept in gaol. Dr Andrew Ure in his *Philosophy of Manufactures* (1835) is reported to have said 'that if children and young persons under eighteen years of age, instead of being kept the full twelve hours in the warm and pure moral air of the factory, are turned out an hour sooner into the heartless and frivolous outer world, they will be deprived, by idleness and vice, of all hope of salvation for their souls'.[1]

Although many schools were founded in the period before 1830 by benevolent people, it is very evident from the discussions on educational problems that the rights of the propertied classes were to be observed. The politicians and the thinkers of the nineteenth century were almost unanimous in considering the education of the lower orders as something apart from that of the middle and upper classes, and while too much importance could not be attached to religious teaching and simple explanations of the 'iron law of wages' in the elementary schools, yet they took no special care to see that these lessons were taught in the public schools or the grammar schools.

The French Revolution with its ideas of liberty, equality and social improvement did much to strengthen Tory feeling in this country against any change, particularly when some English writers, such as Godwin in his *Political Justice* (1793), adopted extreme left wing views. The Reign of Terror and the experiences of French *émigrés* no doubt added to the fears of the English landowning class that the state might play too important a part in the government of the country. Moreover, the fate of the Catholic Church in the early days of the French Revolution made the religious bodies more distrustful of the state.

Benthamism provided the stimulus to use the state and the statutory powers of Parliament to regulate social conditions in accordance with utilitarian principles. There were, of course, many ideas added to Bentham's philosophy by his followers and not all would have been freely accepted by him. Economic theories certainly played an important part. It is no accident that Adam Smith called his book on economics *The Wealth of Nations* (1776). The problem which he considered was the conditions which were most favourable to an increase in national wealth, but although it is an important one, Adam Smith himself realised that it dealt with only one aspect of national life. Before 1750 one concern of government was the breeding of men, and in the quality of men the wealth of nations was measured. By 1830, however, interest had concentrated on the means of increasing the material wealth of the country, and it was assumed that an increase of wealth implied a higher standard of comfort and hence a better race.

Political economy in the nineteenth century was so popular among the educated classes that it reduced the importance of other subjects. Thus political economy showed old problems of finance and social conditions in an entirely new light, and Members of Parliament were keen to apply the new ideas, though their intellectual keenness weakened their human sympathies.

The new economic theories emphasised the production of wealth, and other factors were considered subordinate. 'Labour is the great fact of human life' said *The Times* in 1857, 'and we hesitate to interfere with its sacred obligations unless with the plainest necessity and on behalf of those who cannot help themselves. We should like to know how the newly acquired leisure and the increased wages of our working population are employed now before we take another step in this easy and pleasant, but perhaps downward, direction.'

This emphasis on work was not limited to the duties of the labouring class but also extended to the captains of industry, who were pictured as feverishly struggling for existence against fellow competitors. Increase in the production of wealth was the goal, and in the means of attaining it too little thought was paid to the human beings sweating away their lives for the accumulation of capital for the next generation to enjoy. The method of gaining the maximum of wealth for the national good was to leave industry unfettered, to impose as few state regulations as possible on trade, so that capital could be free to flow in the most profitable channels, and to open the labour market so that capital could be used to the best advantage. *Laissez-faire* never completely dominated the public's view of economics and the idea that state regulation was of some benefit to industry, or at least to national life, was not completely submerged in the new theories of the beneficence of unfettered self interest. Agricultural problems, too, were never regarded by public opinion with the cold logic of the Manchester school of economists, while the development of factory legislation invaded the very castle of the individualist and forced him to turn to humanitarian problems.

There were, however, extenuating circumstances which justify, in part, the materialism of the age. In England in the nineteenth century, labour, owing to its lack of organisation, was the weakest factor in production and, in consequence, wages were reduced to near subsistence level and the hours of labour were long. The rapid increase of population only added to the importance of capital, for a growing population increases the value of the instruments of production, and hence of capital, until the new population has been provided with the necessary tools. This increase in the value of capital led to a rise in the rate of interest and tended to increase savings and to reduce the wages of labour, partly because of the growing town population. Finally, the growth of industry caused new towns to spring up and resulted in the investment of money in building houses for the working classes. Accompanying this there was the displacement of capital from old industries and, where they could not be adapted to the new conditions, it led to a wastage which only increased the cost of new capital. These were the difficulties with which the legislators and the industrialists had to contend, but it cannot be denied that the importance of capital as compared with human worth was increased and not diminished by economic opinion.

The young science of economics was not solely responsible for the attitude of public opinion to the social problems of the age. The French Revolution gave added force to many new ideas but at the same time strengthened the conservative reaction. The philosophers of the late eighteenth century were developing theories of liberty and equality which went far in their criticisms of the existing social contract theories. Godwin in his *Political Justice* put forward a theory of anarchy, and some writers regarded the primitive social state as their ideal. In many shades of thought we find an individualist psychology and a distrust of the state. It is surprising to what extent the radical thinkers of the early nineteenth century believed in the absolute rationality of man. Many realised that their own generation was not absolutely rational, but they hoped that education would ultimately make all men rational.

'So complete was my father's reliance on the influence of reason over the minds of mankind, whenever it is allowed to reach them,' said J. S. Mill in his *Autobiography* (1873), 'that he *felt* as if all would be gained if the whole population were taught to read, if all sorts of opinion were allowed to be addressed to them by word and in writing, and if by means of the suffrage they could nominate a legislature to give effect to the opinions they adopted.'[2] It was not only to politics that this rationalist analysis was applied but to the whole sphere of human psychology. The so-called felicific calculus of Bentham was based on the conception that man was a rational animal who could calculate the quantity of pain or pleasure to be derived from any contemplated action. Man was considered as a purely self-regarding animal devoted to seeking the maximum of pleasure and the minimum of pain.

This rationalist or individualist psychology, was thought to be not only a scientific theory, but also an ethical theory. Here the new individualism derived inspiration from Puritanism and political economy. The ethical theory of Puritanism laid emphasis on personal salvation. Man was a religious animal calculating the good and evil which would stimulate him to action. His desire for personal salvation should be the strongest guiding force in his life and thus he was a self-regarding spirit whose object was Heaven. The Puritan did not make the assumption that man was a rational animal and that with complete rationality the world would reach its ideal. He contemplated the world and society as it was, for the material conditions did not deny the possibility of salvation. Thus the Puritan tended to look at social institutions uncritically. Here the Puritan and the rationalist differed, but the science of political economy reconciled them. Individualism and Puritanism agreed in emphasising the importance of the unit man, political economy accepted the social standards but affirmed that the economic conditions were the subject of inevitable scientific laws and that the free operation of those laws without human impediment would create the best conditions for the individual, either as a rationalist or a Puritan. 'Let there be complete liberty of contract, movement, occupation, trade, throughout the economic world, the greatest body of wealth will be produced and will be distributed in the most serviceable way, everyone getting his proper share, and that too a larger share than he would get in any other way. This is conceived as the true Economic Art based on the Natural Harmony of the individual interests in society, and economic science is devoted to the expounding the laws of wealth in a society so ordered, and incidentally in exposing the follies and fallacies of all existing or proposed obstacles to this system of Natural Liberty.'[3] Such is the summary by J. A. Hobson of the economic theories which were prevalent from 1800 to 1870.

The influence of individualism and economics, and sometimes of Puritanism, was specifically directed to the diminution of the power of the state. The natural harmony which political economy found between selfish and social interests demanded, of course, the maximum scope for the selfish economic interests. The regulation of trade meant the artificial limitation of natural markets; the regulation of the supplies of capital (usury laws) or labour (factory legislation) was an interference with the natural harmony of economic nature and thus prevented the maximisation of wealth. The distribution of wealth between the various producers was again a result of a natural harmony, and any attempt to give one party to production more than its natural share would lead to a diminution of the total amount of wealth produced and hence ultimately of that party's share of the produce. It was all so delightfully logical and was justified by an appeal to nature, to the new scientific laws, to individualist psychology, and even to Puritanism. Individualist psychology was critical of the state because it asserted that each man knew his own interest best. Neither the new economics nor the new psychology argued in favour of anarchy, but the maximum power of government was the minimum necessary for good order.

The individualist argument in favour of the limitation of the sphere of government was strengthened by an appeal to progress. 'All that a wise government could do was to keep as close as possible to the wings of time, to watch his progress and accommodate his motion to their flight': so thought F. Plunket speaking in the House in 1826 on Catholic Emancipation. This appeal to progress was but a thinly disguised defence of expediency, for it is expedient to do what is inevitable and the inevitable is justified by progress. Harriet Martineau, despite her wish for state education and her sympathy with the working classes, was too good a Radical, too convinced of the truth of her political economy and too philosophical an individualist to see the fault of Mr Plunket's analogy and she expressed hearty agreement with it.

Individualist psychology, besides supporting the popular economic theory, also strengthened the movement towards political democracy. Given equality in the rational inheritance of all men and of educational opportunities, then it was a logical conclusion that all men should have equal political rights and duties. This political theory was not consistent, for while it emphasised the rationality of man, it considered that the state, even at its best, was but a result of man's failure to be rational, and that for a race of perfectly rational men a state would be nearly superfluous. Again, the Austinian theory of sovereignty magnified the importance of the state, but the current political theory denied it the capacity to legislate on more than a very limited number of subjects. Thus the sovereign state was limited by theories of economic and political individualism.

This contradiction in rationalist political theory was equalled by the contradiction in theology. To the Protestant, Catholicism was essentially superstitious and neither Church nor the priesthood had any special powers, but his own religion was justified by reason and an appeal to private judgment. Yet when it was suggested that, in the schools for the children of the working classes, only secular education should be given, all belief in reason and the value of private judgment was thrown aside and it was prophesied that infidelity would be the outcome of the Rule of Three, and that a knowledge of the capes and bays of England, in proper rotation, and of the dates of the kings of England, would lead to untold evil without a due admission of creeds, catechisms and Bible readings.

England in the nineteenth century was still emerging from conditions which retained large traces of an earlier and different social system, and there was a mass of law and custom which was obsolete. It proved very difficult to alter the existing law, even when opinion in favour of change was very strong, and thus the idea of limiting the legislative power and regarding it as necessary only for the removal of harmful restrictions was strengthened. The opposition to public administration was even stronger than the feeling against obsolete laws, for as yet the Civil Service was unreformed and local government was held to be essentially corrupt.

In the eighteenth century religion languished and the English Church was almost as much pantheistic as Protestant. By 1830 the Evangelicals in the Church and the Dissenters outside were pursuing an active policy. The Dissenters were eager for the removal of all civil disabilities and some even hoped for the disestablishment of the Church, while the Evangelicals in the Church, their enthusiasm strengthened by the opposition of the Tractarians, were active in vying with the Dissenters for influence in the new industrial districts. Sabbatarian tendencies became marked by 1840 and the Evangelical Sunday became a social institution.

Protestantism was, however, more than a mere outward form; it implied an Individualist theory of society and a dualist philosophy asserting the independence of matter and spirit. The emphasis of Protestantism on individual salvation and individual piety led to two conclusions—the antithesis of mind and matter and the insignificance of social as compared with individual achievement. On the spiritual side, the ultra-refinement of Puritanism led to Calvinism with its band of chosen people who alone gain heavenly bliss, and on the material side to a scientific determinism which readily accepted an individualist psychology, the law of the survival of the fittest, and the bountiful action of competition which was regarded as the foundation of an everlasting and glorious progress.

Puritanism also provided a favourable atmosphere for the reception of the economic theories of the nineteenth century. Indeed, the connection of puritanism with commercialism and industrialism is not limited to nineteenth-century England. The Jews, the most successful race in high finance, are in many ways puritans. Again, the commercial success of the Dutch in the sixteenth and seventeenth centuries coincided with the period of their most rigorous puritanism, though Dutch art triumphed in the same period, and perhaps Cromwellian England and the industrial civilisation of the New England states in America can be cited as similar examples. The somewhat ascetic outlook of puritanism encouraged the ideal of work and in a religion almost devoid of aesthetics, Dutch puritan art excepted, work must tend to be purely material and concerned with the accumulation of wealth alone.

Thus the influence of Puritanism and individualism, of economics and political theory all combined to emphasise the importance of the competitive struggle for wealth. For the puritan the captain of industry showed the virtue of hard work; for the individualist he was the happy man whose self-regarding virtue had maximised his happiness; the economist admired him because he had increased the national wealth and the philosopher because, unlike the state, he was efficient.

Individualist thought was only part of a dominant trend and it was constantly subject to modifying influences. Tory paternalism was still active throughout the period of Benthamism but there emerged also a growing reliance on state regulation and administration. Dicey called this the period of collectivism, dating it from 1865. Some of the writings of J. S. Mill show this trend and also the literary prophets such as Southey, Carlyle and Ruskin. One of Her Majesty's Inspectors of Schools, the Rev. H. Moseley, writing in 1846, said: 'No greater error can be made in elementary education than to suppose that, for the education of the poor man's child, nothing more is required than is needed for our own children.' He explained his idea in a footnote: 'Practically, our elementary education supposes less. We break off a fragment from the education we suppose necessary for our own children—its mechanical and technical part—and give it to the poor man's child in charity. The inveterate prejudice that education in any higher sense is a privilege annexed to a definite social position, and graduated by it, associates itself with all our educational efforts.'[4] This was indeed a very advanced educational ideal for the time.

The development of collectivist ideas implied a faith in state action, but the corruption of administration in the eighteenth century was notorious and the municipal corporations were distrusted. Public administration was condemned for being inefficient where efficiency was required and for interfering when it was efficient in carrying out restrictive legislation. The dislike of public administration, centralisation and municipal corporations explains the marked preference which the law makers of the nineteenth century showed for bodies elected *ad hoc*, such as Schools Boards, Water Boards, Health Boards and Boards of Guardians. One of the new problems of the nineteenth century was the reconciliation of legislation and administration. The new social conditions were beyond the capacity of the old administration and the new social legislation was often ineffective because of the absence of adequate administrative machinery. The appointment of Inspectors was the beginning of some government departments, but at first the Inspectors had often to report their own failure to enforce the law, and frequently the distrust of this minimum of control caused many obstacles to be thrown in their way, so that it was often difficult for them to tell whether the laws were observed or not.

Social legislation before 1870 had prepared the way for the new collectivist trend. When payment of wages was made in kind by employers in certain industries, it was not easy for parents to find the school pence needed for the education of their children, but the Truck Acts (1831, 1887, 1896) improved matters. The Factory Acts of 1833, 1844, and 1867 had restricted the employment of children and in some cases provided for half-time education. The control by the state of the employment of women and children in the mines and factories (Acts of 1819, 1833, 1842 and 1844) was an admission that those unable to fight for themselves needed legal protection, but it took time for an administrative system to be developed which secured adequate enforcement of the laws. Other Acts were passed to protect the workmen—some for arbitration (1867–96), others to give an improved legal status to Trade Unions (1867, 1871, 1875 and 1876) and some to determine Employers' Liability (1880) and the right to Workmen's Compensation (1897). The Education Acts from 1870 are part of this field of social legislation, which aimed at social improvement and not the provision of state systems. It was the rising cost of education, plus the long pockets of the ratepayers, which ultimately led to the decline of the Voluntary Schools and the growth of state control.

The education debates of 1807

It may assist the reader to have some knowledge of the opinions which were current before 1843—the date when this study begins. The education debates of 1807 give a clear view of some of the under-lying social ideas which still existed after 1870. In 1870 such ideas, though they were generally accepted, were not frankly expressed, but in 1807 no one was ashamed of them. In this latter year, Samuel Whitbread introduced into the House of Commons a Bill which attempted to deal with the whole of the Poor Law. The original Bill did not survive long but was divided into four, of which the first part dealt with education. It was proposed to make the parish responsible for the education of the children, and each child was to have two years' education between the ages of seven and fourteen. This was the ideal, which events proved impracticable, of an advanced philanthropist, and two years' schooling was expected to reduce crime and partially to eliminate pauperism. 'But, as he [Whitbread] proposed the education of the poor to be the incipient principle and grand foundation of all the benefits to be derived in future from the measures of reform in the Poor Laws, he thought this Bill, which went peculiarly to that object, should be first established. Education might be said to be the panacea, if anything human could be a panacea, for the ills to which our state was naturally subjected.'[5]

The objections urged against the Bill were many. Some considered the expense was too great and others that it would tend to destroy philanthropic effort. The opposition to the Bill was largely due to the opinion that the several social and economic positions required various degrees of education, and because there was no shortage of clerics, teachers or clerks, there was no need for the education of the lower orders. Mr Simeon, though 'he censured the conduct of those in the higher classes of society, who thought the poor should receive no education . . .' yet himself, 'saw no necessity for writing or arithmetic. He knew of no deficiency in the number of candidates for bankers' clerks and such situations.' Mr Rose 'had no doubt that the poor ought to be taught to read; as to writing, he had some doubt, because those who had learnt to write well were not willing to abide at the plough, but looked to a situation in some counting house'. He also doubted that two years' education would effect much, but 'to carry the system of education to the labouring poor still higher would, he feared, tend rather to raise their minds above their lot in life, and by no means strengthen their attachments to those laborious pursuits by which they were to earn a livelihood; pursuits to which, at present, there existed throughout the poor of this country a very strong reluctance. If, therefore, care was not taken to blend with their education early habits of industry, he feared that schooling would rather injure than serve them, in the result.' Mr Sharpe, a supporter of Whitbread's Bill, 'did not think it possible that education could give sentiments above the condition of the individuals. Education would give habits of industry and attention. He wished for more than two years of instruction; but even in this short period the children, though they should forget all their learning, would have collected many beneficial habits of an indelible nature; habits of submission and respect for their superiors; habits of cleanliness and exertion and the fear of punishment.'

When the supporters of the Bill were so restricted in their outlook, an opponent, Mr D. Giddy, can hardly be blamed for thinking that education would teach the labouring classes of the poor 'to despise their lot in life, instead of making them good servants in agriculture, and other laborious employments to which their rank in society had destined them; instead of teaching them subordination it would render them factious and refractory, as was evident in the manufacturing counties; it would enable them to read seditious pamphlets, vicious books and publications against Christianity; it would render them insolent to their superiors; and, in a few years, the result would be that the legislature would find it necessary to direct the strong arm of power towards them, and to furnish the executive magistrates with much more vigorous laws than were now in force.'[6] In fact, he objected to the Poor Laws *in toto*, because they taxed virtue to help vice. These opinions are explained in part by the fear of the French Revolution, but even more by the belief in a fixed social order in which, it was thought, every one's place could be defined as that position in life to which it pleased God to call him.

The significance of educational changes

It is hoped that this study may help to throw some light on the development of social and political ideas of the period. The student of education may also learn more of the birth pangs which led to the foundation of the modern system of state schools. The story of educational growth may also help to throw a little light on the problems of social and economic history. It is, however, in the field of government that the events related here may be of particular value.

The passing of social services from the control of voluntary bodies to the state is here shown in its early stages. The Poor Law was the only important social duty of the local authorities and the parish unit had already shown itself too small and inefficient to carry out this duty satisfactorily. The Boards of Guardians were formed out of the parish authorities by the Act of 1834, but not until 1868 did the last of the parish authorities for Poor Law administration disappear, and even in 1929 the names of the parishes appeared in the *Streets Book* of the London County Council. The conservatism of the English in retaining the useless parish districts in built-up areas is part of the explanation of the slowness in carrying out administrative reforms. When school attendance was made compulsory in 1880, there were some 2,560 School Boards and 14,200 bodies of school managers with direct access to the Education Authority at Whitehall; no wonder that it took time to carry out administrative reforms. Not until the Acts of 1902 and 1944 were the areas more rationally redrawn. Yet it must be remembered that in 1870 the counties were still under the administration of the Justices of the Peace and had no suitable organs for the administration of a social service.

The town councils were not trusted with the new educational powers and, as with many other new services, *ad hoc* boards were created, though reform came ultimately in 1902, when an Act was passed dissolving the School Boards and giving the powers to the standard local government bodies. Locally elected Boards were retained for the administration of the Poor Law until 1930. One new political idea was applied in the Act of 1870, namely giving each voter as many votes as there were seats to be filled on the School Board. The votes could be given to one candidate or distributed as the voter thought fit. This method of 'proportional representation' did not work well and has not reappeared in any other legislation.

The state's control of education in 1833 was limited to the education of pauper children and some provision for the teaching of the
children of soldiers. The system of parish apprenticeship was used to
teach useful labour to the older children, but this was hardly education in the modern sense. However, the state did not interfere in the
responsibilities of the parishes for their pauper children, except for
the oft-repeated complaint that they should not be mixed with the
adult paupers. For all other children education was a matter for
parental choice, and the lawyers and politicians of the nineteenth
century were reluctant to interfere with well-established principles.
Despite the reforming zeal of a few lawyers there was, in general, a
feeling that unless there was an undoubted evil leading to suffering,
as with the employment of children in the mines, it was unwise to
disturb the existing practice. In the field of secondary education
there was no compulsion until the Education Act of 1944. As is usual
in England, the law lagged behind social opinion; but slow reforms
are certainly easier to administer than advanced ideas which are not
readily welcomed.

A study of this kind also shows the importance of pressure groups in
politics. Roman Catholic Emancipation in 1829, the extension of the
franchise in 1832 and the repeal of the Corn Laws in 1846 owed much
to the pressures of particular groups. In the main one group was able
to claim the success in each of these cases, but with education there
were several pressure groups, some of which had conflicting aims.
They served the purpose of informing public opinion of the new ideas
and more especially of educating Members of Parliament. Some of
the societies also produced statistical reports to prove their arguments
about the quality or quantity of education given to the poor. With the
passing of the Act of 1870 some pressure groups expired, but others
were based on social organisations with a wider purpose, more
particularly those connected with religious bodies. The most important pressure groups were the religious bodies themselves, because of
the large number of schools they controlled or the strength of their
religious zeal for education on some special pattern. In order that a
more national opinion could emerge, it was necessary for impartial
investigations to be made. Today preliminary investigations into the
need for new legislation are often made by Civil Servants at work in
departmental committees, but in the nineteenth century there was
no such reliable body of officials to be trusted with impartial investigations. The Civil Service had not been reformed and the local
government service did not exist, so that Royal Commissions and
Select Committees did much of the work of investigation. They often

relied on men appointed to make special reports for the particular purpose who were not always trained for such work. Nevertheless, these reports helped to frame the ideas which were the basis of subsequent action, whether legislative or administrative. One body of public servants, however, played a most important part in educating public opinion, namely the state Inspectors of Schools. They were in a position to speak with first-hand knowledge, though one must realise that their social outlook was limited as they were mainly recruited from university men and were usually allied to one of the religious bodies.

It was one of the complaints for many years after 1870 that Inspectors were appointed by patronage long after such methods had been replaced in the Civil Service. Being members of the educated class, however, they were listened to at a time when Radical enthusiasts were distrusted and the Inspectors by their annual reports, by letters and articles, by speeches and other means of publicity, drew attention to the need for more radical measures than had been adopted before 1870. The value attached to their reports is shown by the resignation of Robert Lowe from the position of Vice-President of the Committee of Council on Education, because it was said—in error, as it was later shown—that he had been responsible for tampering with the reports of the Inspectors.

It is not possible to develop the theme of the new professional class which began to be formed when the state undertook to encourage the training of teachers. Originally a subordinate group working under the parsons, they have become an educational profession of their own. As in all other European countries they are, unlike parsons, enthusiastic for new ideas. Around the teaching profession has grown a body of educational administrators, school doctors and dentists, school nurses, school architects and suppliers of educational books and apparatus. To the student of public administration this is an important development, as apart from the post office and the armed services there is no other body of official employees so large as that of the educationists.

The teaching profession played another important part in the development of social institutions. Unlike Church of England parsons they were not recruited from a social class intent on persuading the lower orders to recognise their betters. The profession was a way out of the working class or the lower middle class and even before 1870 there was a complaint that some teachers aspired to better things and found a way out of their profession and even became parsons. This did not of necessity mean that they lost their sympathy with the depressed classes, and with their knowledge of social conditions they helped to spread ideas of social reform. The National Union of Teachers became a powerful organisation for spreading the gospel of education.

Administrators and politicians may sometimes think that the hurdles they encounter will never be surmounted, but this account of the history of the ideas leading to the passing of the Education Act of 1870 may give them reason to hope, so long as their cause has sound practical reason on its side, that it may be worth while fighting on. It is, however, necessary not to antagonise those who wander from the argument so that the case becomes bogged down in extraneous issues such as, in this case, religious rivalries, doctrinaire economics, the legal rights of parents under the Common Law or the necessity for teaching secular truth.

REFERENCES

1. Quoted Karl Marx, *Capital*, ed. Swan, p. 211. 1906.
2. J. S. Mill, *Autobiography*, World's Classics edn., p. 89.
3. J. A. Hobson, *Free Thought in the Social Sciences*, p. 75.
4. PP 1846, vol. 32, p. 169.
5. Hans. 24 Apr. 1807, vol. 9, c. 538 and 550.
6. Hans. 24 Apr. 1807, vol. 9, c. 798 and 799.

2

State Interference

Educational societies and state aid

In 1807 the Lord of the Manor of Barton founded a school for forty poor children. 'All the children are to be taught to read but none are to be taught the dangerous arts of writing or arithmetic except such as the lord of the manor shall think fit.' The schools founded for the education of the poor in the eighteenth and nineteenth centuries were often on this model. Charity schools and Sunday schools were inspired by religious motives and any secular education was given in small doses. Yet in the early years of the nineteenth century there was a growing feeling that more should be done to provide schools for poor children. The Royal Lancastrian Association, founded in 1808, became the better-known British and Foreign School Society and by its work many schools were founded, in which secular instruction was given together with religious teaching based on Bible reading; there was a close association with Nonconformity. In contrast, the object of the National Society, founded in 1811, was the promotion of the education of the poor in the principles of the Established Church.

Despite the vigour of these two societies in the building of schools, they proved unable to make a large impression on the number of uneducated children. In 1833 it was estimated that one in eleven of the population attended day school and in the worst slums only one in thirty-five; and at this date children were a larger section of the community because adults died at a comparatively early age. These figures were probably an overestimate because names were kept on school registers after the children had gone or were duplicated on other registers, when families moved. The school buildings were often inadequate, the teachers untrained, many of them quite incompetent; most of the lessons were given by child monitors and the attendance of scholars was very irregular.

The first state grant towards the education of the poor was made in 1833 and for six years its administration was in the hands of the

Treasury. Then in 1839, without any Act of Parliament, the Government announced the formation of a Committee of Privy Council on Education which, despite an adverse vote in the House of Lords of 229 to 118, survived until 1899. Because of the strong opposition of the Church it had to drop its plan for an undenominational state training college for teachers, but it took over from the Treasury the administration of the grants. From 1839 acceptance of the grant gave the government the right to inspect the schools, though the two Societies only agreed grudgingly to inspection. The Privy Council Committee continued to extend its powers by increasing its grants and in 1856 the 'Establishment for the Encouragement of Science and Art,' formerly part of the Board of Trade, came under its control. In this year too a Vice-President for the Committee was authorised by statute and he became the spokesman for education in the Commons. On the other hand, by 1863 it had lost powers to inspect Poor Law and Reformatory Schools which were the original source of inspiration to Sir James Kay-Shuttleworth, the first Secretary to the Committee, in the development of his educational ideas.

The principles laid down in 1833 for the distribution of grants were at the basis of the developments in the next thirty-seven years. The first principle was one of self-help and grants were only made when one-half of the total building expenditure had been raised by voluntary funds. This was modified in 1843 so that extra assistance could be given to schools in poor and populous districts. A capitation grant introduced to help rural schools in 1853 and extended to all schools in 1856, was only given when the income from private sources exceeded 12s per head in girls schools and 14s in boys schools. The children also had to pay between 1d and 4d a week as school fees, so that none of the poorest schools could hope to qualify for these grants.

It became evident to the Inspectors from the beginning that the use of child monitors was a failure. They could only teach by rote and when too many were employed, which was often done for the sake of economy, the discipline of the school was undermined. This led the Privy Council Committee to take an interest in the training of teachers and by the Minutes of 1846 children of thirteen were encouraged to become apprentices—or pupil teachers as they became known—for a period of five years for a small salary. The pupil teachers were only allowed in schools approved by the Inspectors and where the head teacher was a suitable person to give instruction. For this reason pupil teachers in Ragged Schools were not accepted. 'The position of the pupil teacher is a public one, and my Lords think it should be understood . . . to be a prize for the children of independent parents who make sacrifices to educate them properly.'[1] Every year the pupil teacher was examined by the Inspector. At age eighteen the best pupil teachers were encouraged by scholarships to go to a teachers' training college, but those who did not enter were accepted as assistant teachers. The trained teacher at the end of two years sat for his certificate and a certificated teacher was accepted as a qualified person to train pupil teachers. Government payments were made to pupil teachers, the head teachers who trained them, and to the college trained teachers; in addition, the greater part of the cost of the training colleges was paid for by the government. In this way a supply of teachers was obtained without much expense with a certain guarantee of teaching ability. In the whole field of public administration there is no comparable example of a successful training system.

By 1852 more than half the annual grant for education was being spent on teachers and teacher training. This was a departure from the principle of self-help but the capitation grants were based on the self-help idea and were made conditional on the employment of certificated teachers.

By 1858 expenditure by the state on education was so considerable that there was a demand for investigation, and the Newcastle Commission (1858–61) made some unfavourable comments on the system. Robert Lowe, then Vice-President of the Committee of Privy Council, published his Revised Code to reduce chaos to order and abolished all the annual grants to schools, to teachers and to pupil teachers, authorising one grant in their place; this was paid to the schools managers and was based on examination results.

The idea of an examination of the children was not new, as it formed part of the Minute of 1853 on the capitation grant, but the annual grant was now a question of payment by results. The maximum grant was based on the other income of the school. This still meant that the poorer schools had no hope of qualifying for the grant. Building grant rules were unchanged and the parents still had to pay 1d to 4d per week. Schools had to employ certificated teachers and the Inspectors' approval was needed.

Grants under the Treasury Minute of 1833 were limited to the schools of the National Society and the British and Foreign School Society, and both made religious teaching the basis of education. In 1839 the rule was made 'that no plan of education ought to be encouraged in which intellectual instruction is not subordinate to the regulation of the thoughts and habits of the children by the doctrines and precepts of revealed religion'.[2] This opened the door to other societies: Roman Catholics received the grant in 1847 and Jews in

1852, but grants to secular schools were refused until 1870. The Privy Council Committee framed a conscience clause to protect children from proselytism, particularly in districts with only one school.

It is clear from the principle of self help that the schools were intended for the respectable poor. If parents paid more than 4d per week then the school could not qualify for grant, but some complaints were made in 1870 that better-class children whose parents could afford full costs at private schools were attending state-aided schools, which no doubt proved the superiority of the teaching. The parent who paid 1d to 4d per week was more likely to ensure regular attendance and a modicum of cleanliness. The more penurious parents, when they found a child was unable to go to school on Monday kept it at home all the week to save the fee. (This was still true at the free-charging Voluntary Schools of the early twentieth century.) Children at the bottom of the social ladder were taught in the workhouse, or in the Industrial and Reformatory schools, or even in prison. Some philanthropists thought this was not enough and started Ragged Schools for neglected children or those whose parents were too poor to pay for schooling. Despite the efforts of social workers, including Lord Shaftesbury, Charles Dickens and Miss Burdett Coutts, they were usually unable, except for a few short years from 1857 to 1862, to qualify for the full grant. The Privy Council Committee said that Ragged Schools must confine themselves to the free education of children belonging to 'that class which cannot be associated with the children of respectable labouring men', because, as the official reports of 1852–3 say, such schools tend to weaken the sense of parental responsibility in the labouring class. In most of these schools some industrial work was done, if only to help in meeting the cost, but in Reformatory Schools one Inspector recommended solitary confinement with bread and water for the worst children.

In Poor Law schools some improvement was reported, and in 1856 one of them had classes in instrumental music. The Inspector said this training was good but 'some persons have objected to teaching boys of this class instrumental music, under the erroneous idea that it may lead to dissipation'. In 1859 it was reported that only a few Guardians continued the policy of giving the children very little exercise because of the wear and tear on the clothes and the effect on the appetite. Religious teaching, said an Inspector in 1849, was of course given in the Poor Law schools; 'Education is in all cases fruitless without it; but it is especially so with pauper children who possess a larger share than common of the natural sin and evil habit to which all flesh is heir.'[3]

Besides the work of the Committee of Privy Council the various religious bodies played a considerable part in furthering the cause of education and their work will be considered in Chapter 3. The Central Society of Education, founded in 1836, issued a quarterly journal which helped to emphasise the need for more schools. It was supported by leading Whigs and Liberal members of Parliament and for some years played a fairly important part; it was even powerful enough to embarrass the government in 1839. More active in politics was the Lancashire Public School Association, founded in 1847, which changed its name to the National Public School Association in 1850. Richard Cobden was one of its members and was able to take an active part once the Corn Law problem was settled in 1846. The Association's policy comprised free schools supported by local rates, managed by locally elected committees, with secular education only because of the religious difficulty. It unsuccessfully promoted Bills in Parliament and made its ideas well known. The Manchester and Salford Committee was a society with similar aims, except that it wished for comprehensive religious teaching. The popularity of education among some philanthropic people led to a new society being formed in 1857, which continued for three years before it was found to be fraudulent.

In 1869 two further societies were formed—the Education League and the National Education Union; the former turned to a secularist policy after 1870, while the latter represented Anglicanism and Conservatism. The Act of 1870 was in part the result of the work of these two groups, whose work will be described in more detail in Chapter 6, but once the Act had been put into operation, much of their raison d'être had gone and they soon vanished from the scene.

Factory legislation

What of the children for whose benefit the schools were being built? Gulliver in his travels found that 'cottagers and labourers keep their children at home, their business being only to till and cultivate the earth, and therefore their education is of little consequence to the Publick'. Swift's opinion in 1726 was still common a hundred years later. The parson had an interest in church attendance and therefore favoured schools in which religious instruction was given, but little else. The state only interfered where it was not in conflict with parental authority. The parent was free to send his child to work at any age except in a few factories after 1833 and in the mines after 1842. Cruelty to children was not the subject of specific legislation till 1889.

The Poor Law made provision for pauper apprentices and by the Factory Act of 1802 some protection was given to these children and a certain minimum of education prescribed. This Act was evaded and its educational results were negligible. A further Factory Act of 1819 prohibited the employment of children under nine in certain factories, but without birth certificates and factory inspectors the Act was a dead letter. The Factory Act of 1833 authorised the employment of factory inspectors, but they had little control over the educational clauses. The Act of 1844 was the most successful, but it only applied to certain factories and to children between eight and thirteen years. Its effect in some cases was to drive children from such factories. By 1867 the Factory Acts had been extended to cover most children in industry, but they did not cover the whole child population.

Building standards

Laws, minutes and regulations can only provide the foundations on which school managers and teachers must build. School building, which today has become a specialised department of architecture, was of a very low standard. Government minutes about building standards were difficult to enforce, since it often seemed better to accept poor buildings, hoping for improvement, than to deny the grant knowing that the school would otherwise very likely go down hill. Even good schools could become inadequate if their classes became overfull or if, as a result of trade depression, the fortunes of the school changed completely. The death of a benefactor or the appointment of a new headmaster could make or break a school.

Training of teachers

It was as difficult to secure good teachers as to build good schools. For some years after the Minutes of 1846 there was a serious shortage of teachers and the pupil teacher system could not expand until there was a sufficient number of good teachers to train the young hopefuls. There was no adequate system of secondary schools which could be used for training pupil or student teachers until well after 1900. By 1856 it was possible for the Government to insist on trained teachers, even if they were only partly trained ex-pupil teachers who had not been to college. The cost of employing fully trained teachers as assistants was for most schools prohibitive and pupil teachers did the bulk of the work. The Government tried to prevent the abuse of the system and limited the number to four pupil teachers per trained teacher, but not before one Inspector had reported finding twelve in one school. The improvement in teaching received an unconscious tribute from one child who, when asked: 'Why did the eunuch go away rejoicing?' frankly replied: 'Please, sir, because Philip had a' done a'teaching on him.'

The curriculum of the schools was very limited and many children barely acquired the elements of reading, writing and arithmetic. This was a principal complaint of the Newcastle Commission, which found in some schools a tendency for teachers to neglect the bulk of children who were backward and to teach the best the more fancy subjects, which to the teacher were more interesting. The Revised Code of 1861, by its principle of payment by results, did improve the work of the lower standards, but at such an educational cost that no one had a good word to say about its results.

Parents and children

The imperfections of the schools were equalled by the imperfections of the pupils and parents. Children arrived at times best suited to their families and registers often had to be kept open all morning. Some children left school early to take father's lunch to the factory. The Inspectors hoped this would be remedied when the Capitation Grants were introduced, but they were disappointed. School managers, in their efforts to qualify for the grant, were afraid to insist on punctuality, cleanliness and good behaviour in case they lost income from the grants. It was suggested that the only remedy was to define an attendance for capitation purposes as five hours. The legalised irregularity of the factory children added to the difficulties of the teachers.

The period of school life rarely exceeded three years from eight to eleven, and even then many children moved from school to school. Sometimes this was due to changes of address but also, with a fee-paying system, parents often felt they were conferring a benefit on the school, and if the child was punished they were ready to send him elsewhere in the town. Payment of fees also led to irregular attendance. If the parent was short of money and the school insisted on regular payments, the child stayed away. One unexpected side effect was the tendency of teachers to pay more attention to those who paid higher fees for tuition in extra subjects; this made the parents of other children discontented. The Capitation Grants and the Revised Code both aimed at giving financial stimulus to better work and better attendance, but until education became compulsory and free, irregular attendance was always a problem.

It is these qualitative considerations which make it so difficult to understand the schools statistics of the period. These are sometimes quoted with great aplomb to prove one or another educational theory. The figures of the Newcastle Commission were in the main based on detailed returns from a few selected areas. Since even the detailed returns took no account of potential errors or the qualitative factors mentioned above, it is clear that the national figures are not reliable, except to show the very broadest trends.

In these days of hasty legislation too little credit is given to the Victorians for their foresight. Sir James Kay-Shuttleworth, the energetic secretary of the Committee of Privy Council on Education when it was first formed, was fully aware of the great difficulties in educating the people as a result of his other social investigations, particularly as a Poor Law Assistant Commissioner. He planned first to increase the number and quality of school teachers and school buildings and the laws for compulsory education would have been a dead letter without his careful preparation. Although he was unable to carry on as secretary after 1849, he never lost his interest in the cause, and by correspondence, publications and personal influence he continued to exercise a pressure on public opinion which helped to build up the idea of a national scheme of education for all children. In some respects we may think that his aims were low, in that education was conceived on a class basis, but he could hardly have been a successful administrator if he had adopted ideas too far in advance of his generation. What he would have done if faced with the planning of Piccadilly Circus we cannot tell, but he was always prepared to make a cautious advance in another direction if faced with an impasse.

REFERENCES

1. PP 1852–3, vol. 79, pp. 50–1.
2. PP 1841, vol. 20, p. 100, Instructions to Inspectors, 1840.
3. PP 1849, vol. 42, p. 593.

3

3

The Religious Conflict

In these days of religious neutrality, or even indifference, it is difficult
to imagine the bitterness of feeling 120 years ago about the problem
of religious education. Yet as recently as 1927 there were very
acrimonious debates in the House of Commons about the adoption of
the Revised Prayer Book, in which the votes of the evangelical
M.P.s defeated the proposals supported by the bishops and the House
of Lords. The Protestant opponents regarded the measure as a step to
Rome and it is significant that this cry should have raised such strong
feeling. Today there would be no argument, though political parties
are loth to raise religious issues which might burn their fingers. In the
nineteenth century, and even in the education debates of the Parlia-
ments of 1900–14, indifference and neutrality were considered a sign
of atheism or near paganism, and the temperature of the education
debates easily became very heated. Lord Brougham even went so far
as to say in August 1854, that 'the Odium Theologicum seems like
gravitation, only that it is repulsive and not attractive, to act inversely
as the distance, or even in a higher proportion to the proximity of faith'.

In the early years of the nineteenth century the position of the
Established Church was undisputed; it was a partner of the state in all
matters which affected religion. Nonconformists, created by the Act
of Uniformity of 1662, had gradually received some degree of toleration, but not of equality. They played a small part in politics and
some historians say that this diverted their energies to success in the
economic concerns of the nation and the manufacturing industries of
the growing towns. The Roman Catholics were almost outside the
pale, and even in the early part of the twentieth century, in the public
elementary schools of Merseyside, children did not treat Roman
Catholics as fellow pupils, perhaps because they were usually Irish as
well as Catholic.

Despite the social and political inferiority of those who did not
belong to the Church of England they were becoming more self

assertive about their rights. The Acts passed in the last years of the reign of George IV gave Nonconformists and Roman Catholics political rights and from then on they fought for more and more recognition. Every political proposal which seemed to favour the Church of England was a retrograde step which threatened their hard won victories against the Establishment.

The duty of educating the people had always been a religious one and the Church of England had control of education in all state schools, be they Poor Law, Army or prison schools. Samuel Whitbread's Education Bill of 1807 recognised no other Church than the Established Church. The teaching of the Church was a bulwark of the state; it taught due obedience to the laws and to public authority and it also taught the wealthy to be philanthropic and to assist in the religious education of the poor. As one writer put it, the parson and the devil were the cheapest policemen; but the Noncomformist minister and the Catholic priest were suspect because they might preach in favour of amending the law. In the troublous times of 1842 it was said that there were fewer riots in districts where Church education was strongest.

Although the Church was bolstered by the state, and vice versa, its influence was weakened by the growing division among its members. The Wesleyans and Methodists began the exodus from the Church. Later the Tractarians, or Puseyites as they were sometimes called by contemporaries, raised another minority movement and the defection of some of its members to the Roman Catholic Church led to accusations of Papistry, which to Nonconformists and the evangelical sections of the Church itself, was a rallying cry. The High Churchmen remained opponents of the educational policy of the state even after 1870, but the moderate Churchmen were hopeful of government aid when the Tories were in office, though decidedly suspicious when Whigs or Liberals were in power. The Nonconformists owed to Peel and his reluctant Tory supporters the Act of 1828 which gave them political equality and they hoped that the Whig Reform Act of 1832 would strengthen their influence, as more Nonconformists than Churchmen would get the vote. The Whigs in 1836 relieved Dissenters from the obligation of being married in Church imposed by the Marriage Act of 1753, though a further Act was necessary in 1898 to make the presence of the Registrar superfluous at all Nonconformist Chapel weddings. In the universities the dissenters did not achieve equality until late in the century; they also argued that the payment of Church rates was unjust. It seemed to them that only through Parliament could they consolidate their position, more particularly when the Whigs were in office. The Roman Catholics also hoped for an improvement in their position, and in 1848 the Whig Government would have won support for a Bill to re-establish diplomatic relations with the Pope but for the revolutions in Europe.

The religious conflict on education was embittered by the support which many eminent men gave to the policy of secular education. Agnosticism and the French Revolution were considered as cause and effect, but there was a growing number of serious minded men, particularly among the Radicals, who were agnostics, though the flippant atheism of the Frenchman had no support among English agnostics such as J. S. Mill. The agnostics, however, like the Nonconformists and the Catholics, looked to the state to carry out educational reforms and this heightened the suspicions of Churchmen when the state tried to extend its powers to control schools for the working class. The Churchmen expected that state interference in education would lead to the growth of immorality and the decay of religion; and who are we in the 1960s to say that they were wrong?

Denominationalism and secularism

The idea of secular education was never popular in the thirty years before the Education Act of 1870. Even those who preferred unsectarian education were often condemned as secularists, although they wanted Bible teaching in the schools. The debates were thus confused and raised considerable passions. Henley said in the House of Commons in May 1855 that the establishment of an educational system which was 'religious in name alone, but sure ere long to become purely secular' would be 'contrary to the direct command of God, who has pointed out to us in the clearest manner, from Genesis to Revelation, that Life is not to be gained through the tree of knowledge'. Another M.P. in the debate on 22 May 1851, quoted the words of an evangelical clergyman, saying: 'The more a man is advanced in human knowledge, the more he is opposed to religion, and is the more deadly enemy to the truth of God.' At a diocesan meeting in 1860 Gathorne Hardy, who introduced the Bill for free education in 1891, said: 'Without religion he would rather see no education at all; Knowledge was good but wisdom was better; and without religion they could not get wisdom. The fear of the Lord is wisdom, and to depart from it is not understanding.'[1]

To such arguments W. J. Fox, a Unitarian minister and a leading secularist, said in Parliament in June 1850, that he denied 'the impious assumption that men could be led away from religion by studying the works of the Creator'. In a debate in May the following year he said: 'It seemed as though there were something evil in knowledge', in the eyes of his opponents, 'which required to be counteracted by even bad theology; that history was not to be studied unless it was accompanied by heresy; and that decimal fractions were fatal to the soul if they were not mingled with that which some called idolatry.'

There was of course a distinction between subjects which might have a religious bearing and others devoid of religious significance; 'no man', averred Mr Adderley, 'asked his dancing master to fiddle and teach religion to his children at the same moment'. On the other hand 'mere reading and writing did not make a good man, nor scientific acquirements a moral man', said Mr Borthwick in 1846, 'education wrongfully imparted had only the tendency of making the criminal a more clever criminal''[2] a sentiment with which the modern safe-breaker would no doubt agree. In fact the amount of crime showed that there was a greater need for religious as opposed to secular education and to this the secularists replied that the existing religious education was, evidently, a proven failure. A child who had learnt his secular knowledge at a day school, said Earl Russell in December 1857, would make a better pupil at the Sunday school, and therefore secular education aided religious education. The majority of secularists were members of a church, but they saw in secular education the only hope of achieving a national system of schools. *The Times* in an article of 27 February 1850 used the analogy of Eton, where religion formed only a small part of the whole, to condemn the exclusively religious education for the poor. 'It was only when education was to be given to the poor', said W. J. Fox in the House of Commons in May 1851, 'when it was to be administered as a sort of charity, that religion was inculcated, not for its own benign-ant influence, but for the sake of keeping them in order and tran-quility; and then it was that such a preponderance was given to theology'.[3] An Inspector for Roman Catholic schools in the north of England wrote in his official report of 1860 that religious teaching was the one bright spot in the prevailing gloom. The priests calm 'the disturbed and dissatisfied by lessons of obedience and resignation, and training generations of suffering children to endure with patience the social pressure to which they are exposed; indeed, I can verify that the clergy to whom I refer answer the purpose of the most efficient peace officers'.[4] To many the only possible hope of a national system was a secular system whereby the religious differences would be overcome, but to others this was an argument which proved the

27

absurdity of proposing any national system, because the religious bodies could not be excluded from the schools which they had themselves provided.

Secularism was in decline between 1855 and 1866. The success of the system of grants in encouraging the building of new schools and the inclusion of Jews and Roman Catholics in the scheme made it seem unlikely that a secular policy would succeed. Almost alone in the House of Commons Sir John Pakington, the Conservative educationist, pressed for a national system with unsectarian religious teaching, and though his Education Bills failed, he was successful in 1858 in securing the appointment of a Royal Commission on Education, later known as the Newcastle Commission. During the three years when it collected evidence, the state of education was not very actively discussed in Parliament. Following the introduction of the Revised Code in 1861 for the allocation of grants, which originated from the Newcastle Commission Report, the merits and defects of the Code were the main subject of educational debate and the religious issue did not become important until 1866, when it became likely that some nationwide legislation would be necessary. Then the secular theme was again vigorously debated, but despite the hopes of its Christian and non-Christian supporters it could not prevail against those who preferred 'the exacerbated antagonisms of religious tenets to the lukewarm notions of a common Christianity',[5] as Lord Robert Montagu said in Parliament in March 1870. The ultimate success of the unsectarian policy by 1944 was the result of administrative developments rather than deliberate governmental policy. The indifference to religious teaching by 1944, the Roman Catholics excepted, made even an unsectarian policy seem acceptable.

Churchmen and dissenters

The evangelical movement in the Church in the late eighteenth century led in the end to the breakaway groups of Wesleyans and Methodists, but at the same time it brought new vigour to the existing Nonconformist Churches. This in its turn led to a reaction from which the High Church party sprang in the 1830s. 'The repeal of the Test and Corporation Acts in 1828 seemed to remove the chief obstruction in the way of a general school system', said Lord Brougham in July 1854, but in fact it increased the difficulties. Horace Mann in his report on the census of 1851 estimated that nearly half of the population of England and Wales were Dissenters. There was a considerable increase in the number of Roman Catholics due to the immigration of Irish labour, particularly in the years 1845–7 following the Irish famine. The Report of the Newcastle Commission in 1861 showed that 76 per cent of children in schools attended Church of England schools but only 46 per cent attended their Sunday Schools, from which it could be argued, though not conclusively, that some 30 per cent of the Dissenters' children were subject to Church of England pressures. Yet contemporaries were very ill-informed on the subject, and the Bishop of Oxford in July 1850 said dissenters only numbered one-eighth of the population. Dissenters were more active in the towns, and therefore the problem of educating factory children and street urchins was more especially their concern. The Church of England had its strongholds in the rural parishes, and through its wealth and influence, its dominant position in the two leading universities and in Parliament it could always rely on solid support for its cause.

The position of the dissenters was a weak one because of their many divisions. They had no Church rates or endowments to help them and in the main their members, particularly the Roman Catholics, were not as wealthy as the Anglicans. Although the Reform Act of 1832 strengthened their position, this only made the Church more anxious than ever not to yield an inch lest it should lose a yard.

The disunity among the dissenters was paralleled by some disunity among Anglicans, although they had one leader in the Archbishop of Canterbury. The Tractarians, as the High Churchmen were at first called, were opposed to the religious policy of the state, which showed more and more toleration of dissent. On the other hand, the Evangelicals within the Church, such as Lord Shaftesbury, were inclined at times to work with the Nonconformists.

When the Whig Government of 1839 appointed the Committee of Privy Council on Education to control the grants formerly administered by the Treasury, there was violent opposition by Tories and Churchmen, particularly against the scheme for an undenominational training college for teachers. In the House of Lords the Archbishop of Canterbury moved six resolutions condemning the Government, and he secured a vote in his favour of 229 to 118. In the Commons the Government only won a similar debate by five votes, but it decided that it could not carry through its training college scheme. The Committee of Privy Council, with its very able secretary Dr James Kay (later Sir James Kay-Shuttleworth), weathered the storm and began negotiations with the National Society and the British and Foreign School Society to appoint government Inspectors of Schools (somewhat on the model of the Factory Inspectors under the Factory Act of 1833) to ensure that grants were being well used.

The storm of 1839, when the Tories fought the Whig Government proposals, should have been a warning to Sir Robert Peel when the education clauses of the Factories Bill were being prepared in 1842. There had been negotiations with the Church of England, which was not entirely in favour of the Bill because of its concessions to the dissenters; but when the Bill was debated in the House, so strong was the opposition of the Nonconformists in the country that despite the successful vote on the second reading the Bill was withdrawn. In 1844 when it reappeared, the disputed education clauses were left out.

The Nonconformists particularly objected to the Bill because of the composition of the boards of trustees for the schools. The minister and two churchwardens were to be *ex officio* members and the other four appointed by the J.Ps from those assessed to the poor rate or from substantial contributors to the school; they were to include two occupiers of factories. Because of the opposition of the Nonconformists an amendment was made to include only one churchwarden and to strengthen the vote of school subscribers.

The clauses which dealt with religious teaching gave even more offence, for the schoolmaster had to be a member of the Church of England, and the children, except those whose parents objected, were to be taught the catechism and parts of the liturgy, and were to attend divine service on Sundays and some other days. Since Nonconformists' children were more likely to be in a majority in the factory areas, this was an added reason for their opposition. When amended, the Bill set aside three hours on one day of the week when religious instruction could be given to the non-Anglican children.

The Nonconformists and the Roman Catholics continued to fight against the Bill even after its amendment. Meetings were held all over the country and the number of petitions against the Bill exceeded all precedent. Within the House opposition was slight, but Sir Robert Peel felt that, even though the Bill were passed, it might be difficult to administer because of local opposition.

Lord Ashley wrote to Peel, saying: 'We must ascribe much—very much—of the resistance to the fears of the people caused and stimulated by the perilous pranks of Dr Pusey and his disciples. A vast body of Churchmen actuated by these alarms rejoiced in the opposition.' If the Bill had become law it is unlikely that there would be more than 35,000 factory school places and therefore its religious effect would have been negligible; but the result of the failures of 1839 and 1843 was to make all Governments afraid of general legislation.

Between 1843 and 1867 there was only one Government Bill aiming at a national system of education and this only applied to the Boroughs.

The failure of the 1843 Bill is not to be regretted so much as the display of bitter religious feeling is to be deplored. If the churches had shown any ability to co-operate in solving a real social problem, as had been done in other countries including the U.S.A., then there might have developed at an earlier date a truly national system. As it was, all Peel could say in July 1844, after the storm died down, was that 'the jealousy manifested with respect to public education had its evils ... but it showed an independent spirit which ought to be respected'. Sir James Graham, in the concluding debate on 15 June 1843, speaking as the Home Secretary in charge of the Bill, even found the Church at fault because it had not given the Bill cordial support. It is more than possible that if the dissenters had not fought so hard there would have been stronger opposition from Churchmen, particularly the Tractarians.

The Nonconformists were so elated with their success in defeating the Bill that an association was formed shortly afterwards for the disestablishment of the Church. 'We [the Nonconformists] have at any rate prevented a gorged and tyrannical priesthood from laying hold on the minds of youth, snatching from them all hopes of Christian liberty, and dragging them back into the darkness of the middle ages ...'—so said a report in *The Times* of 11 January 1844, about a speech of the Rev. J. Aldiss at a meeting in the Old Kent Road. The violence of this statement may be compared with the words of the *Church Times* on 25 February 1870; 'Thanks to the persistent roguery of the shop-keeping interest since it went Nonconformist and left off learning its catechism, we have at last No. 1 of a FOOD JOURNAL, devoted in great measure to the detection and exposure of adulteration and other knaveries of this kind.'

The High Church party made much show of its sacrifices in not opposing the Bill of 1843. Sir Robert Inglis, Member for the University of Oxford, said in March 1843 that he claimed 'for the Established Church the maintenance of her office as the supreme instructress of the people of this country ... he was fully aware of the concessions which the Church was making to a plan of national education which did not recognise the Church as the instructress of the people'.[6] *The Times* on 10 June 1844, said: 'The Government has long been struggling to purloin from the Church the education of the country.' Even in the next decade, Mr Drummond said in the House in April 1856: 'It is the Church alone, after their parents, which God ordained to educate the youth of a nation.'

The High Churchmen were critical of the status of the Inspectors, first appointed in 1840, and they tried unsuccessfully to make them less dependent on the Committee of Privy Council and more responsible to the National Society; but Dr Kay circumvented their plans. In 1847 the Whig Government insisted on the cooperation of laymen in the management of schools, and limited the authority of the bishops in appeals from the managing committees. This gave offence to the High Church party and some of the more extreme members severed their schools from the state system and refused to admit the Inspectors. They wished to maintain the authority of the priest and to be free to select the form of trust deed suited to their own ideas. Again, the Government wished to safeguard the position of the Nonconformists who, in many one-school areas, had to attend the Church schools. The Conscience Clause was approved by the government with this end in view; it was condemned by the High Church party, and in many instances it was evaded. It was not unusual to find Nonconformist children excluded from school treats and similar functions.

In time most of the High Churchmen accepted the Government grants, although one M.P. among their supporters considered the Committee of Privy Council to be an anomalous body because no one member was of necessity a member of the Church of England, as Hansard reports on 24 March 1843. On the other hand a few, led by the Rev. G. A. Denison, Archdeacon of Taunton and brother of a Speaker of the House of Commons, continued to do battle and used violent words and extreme language. 'The Church may not ... minister to the delusion that the reading of the Bible is the same thing with teaching and learning religious truth; nor do anything to compromise the principle that, without the steady inculcation of dogma, school teaching is no blessing to parent or child, but the reverse.'[7] A year earlier he said in *The Times* of 12 November 1866; 'A clergyman of the Church of England has, first, to educate the children of the Church in the principles of the Church of England basing all his teaching upon, and leavening it throughout, with these principles. This is his proper business in his school. If he sees his way into admitting into that school the children of Dissenters, as very many do, in order to bring them to be Church children, that is his second business. But it is not and can never be his business to have children in his school to whom he can either teach no religion, or such religion as is not the religion of the Church of England.'[8] The High Churchmen continued their opposition to state education and the English Church Union, their organisation, opposed the Education Act of 1870.

The success of the Nonconformists in defeating the Factory Bill of 1843 surprised them, and this raised their hopes for further advance towards religious equality. Edward Miall, a former Nonconformist minister, organised in 1844 an Anti-State Church Association, and about the same time the Congregational Board of Education and the Voluntary School Association were formed. The Catholics, Wesleyans, Methodists and smaller groups accepted Government aid and inspection, but the Congregationalists, Baptists and some others stood out for a long time against any form of Government aid or inspection. Homerton Training College was run by them independently for their own teachers.

The Voluntaryists, as they were called, were not opposed to the education of the masses but they insisted that religion was the first element in education. If the state gave any support to denominational schools it was using public money to support error as well as truth—since only one religious sect could be teaching the truth—and hence state aid was fundamentally wrong. 'No civil ruler is justified . . . in enforcing the teaching of religion . . . and compelling universal payment for it, by making the Socinian pay towards Roman Catholic doctrines and Roman Catholics towards doctrines they deem heretical and all parties made to aid, by compulsory payment, the spread of error and truth.' They also objected to state aid on political grounds: 'I have no wish to impute any sinister design, but many men about the Government avow the policy of getting the mind of the nation under an unitive system of education. . . . They would bid for all influence—the Pulpit and the Press; they would buy up all priesthoods and fellowships. They would torture all into shape and fix that shape for ever. It is against such a Machiavellian, Austrian, Chinese archetype that we contend.' [9]

State education, it was argued, limited the freedom of parents and demoralised them by denying their rights and taking over their responsibilities. Yet it was said in the House by Mr Barnes in June 1856, 'that the monster difficulty which stood in the way of the spread of education among the children of this country was the indifference of parents whether their children were educated or not'. He also argued that the existing system of education through state aid stood condemned because it failed 'to refine the tastes, raise the morals, and remove the ignorance of the people'. Free education would remove from the parent the incentive to send his child to school and get his money's worth. Parents, he thought, could well afford to pay the school fees; 'Now would anyone say that the bulk of the working people of this country were not in a condition to afford the price of one pint of beer a week for the education of each of their children ?'[10] As for compulsory education, it was said that 'liberty is more precious than education; that education could be no counterbalance to the disturbance of any right; that the reluctant parent, embittered by the violence, would thwart any contingent good; that the deported, abducted child would participate the parental rancour, and nurse his little revenge, and that this would be a civil war to the very hearth. We do not believe that, whatever pains be taken to blind and corrupt the people, the nation's heart will ever be so craven and so sunk to endure the indignity.'[11] 'Education votes were no more than moral poison to prevent the healthy action of the public spirit of the country', said one M.P. when the Education Vote was being discussed on 18 April 1855.

The Voluntaryists asserted that the success of the voluntary system was already proved and there was no need for Government action. Parents were able and willing to provide for their children's education and there was no serious deficiency. The 450 million letters sent annually through the post office, said Hadfield on 6 March 1856, proved that the lower classes were not uneducated. In a debate on 21 June 1858 Gilpin argued that 'ample means for the education of the people would be provided by voluntary agency, as fast as and faster than the people were prepared to desire it and avail themselves of it'. Edward Baines, jnr, the chief spokesman for the party and editor of the *Leeds Mercury*, said in July 1859, that he 'was anxious for the spread of education. He verily believed, however, that they would find it best to leave education, like industry, to a system of perfect freedom.' Three years earlier Barnes had said that 'the money voted by Parliament for the purpose of educating the humbler classes was wholly misapplied, and the benefit of it was given altogether to a different class of people, who did not want the money'.[12]

Statistics were readily produced by the Voluntaryists to prove their arguments. It was maintained that the government grants paid 28 per cent of the total spent on school accommodation but that the surplus accommodation was more than 28 per cent of the whole and the grants were superfluous. There was also a greater increase in the number of scholars in the period 1818–33, when there were no Government grants given, than in 1833–51. The largely increased grants after the 1847 Minutes were not doing much good because the increase in the number of scholars at National schools was greater in the decade 1837–47, although it was admitted that the standard of education and the qualifications of teachers had shown improvement. Yet Baines argued in the debate on 22 July 1859 that the state should not undertake the education of schoolmasters any more than of any other class, such as lawyers, medical men, authors, editors or farmers. Two years later he said that a greater proportion of children were being educated in England than in Holland or France; 'Surely these facts ought to induce them to consider whether it was necessary to maintain the present system to its full extent, whether Government interference could not, at least in some degree, be withdrawn, and whether education could not be safely left to the spontaneous efforts of the people?' The argument is not unfamiliar to readers of the book *Education and the State* by Dr E. G. West, published in 1965. The Voluntaryists refused to give evidence to the Newcastle Commission even though one of their number was a member.

In 1867 the Voluntaryists admitted the failure of their policy. They had failed to unite all Nonconformists and even all the Baptists and Congregationalists had not joined forces with them. The Wesleyans had been persuaded by Lord Ashley to accept the conditions of the Minutes of 1847 and the Roman Catholics and the Jews also realised their hopes of state aid. The one idea which united the Voluntaryist party was their opposition to state-supported religion. The same reaction occurred among some leading Nonconformists when the Education Act of 1902 was passed, but then, while state grants were thought innocuous, it was only rate aid which was thought pernicious. Baines said in the House in July 1861 that he 'did not believe that the Founder of our Faith intended his doctrines should be inculcated by compulsory taxation'. Underlying all this was the feeling that the system of state aid was doing more for the Church of England than for the Nonconformists in proportion to the taxes paid by each. The argument produced by writers of a later generation, that the religious neutrality of the Committee of Privy Council favoured the Non-conformists because they preferred undogmatic religious teaching, was not seriously advanced in the period of 1843–70.

Schools which were entirely dependent for their income on fees and voluntary contributions soon found that their income fluctuated too much for efficiency to be maintained. The great advantage of the government grant before 1862 was that it could be relied upon to pay a definite share of the expenses every year. Although Congregationalists maintained their own training college at Homerton without Government aid or inspection, a similar college in Wales became a private venture college dependent on fees.

When Baines recanted in 1867, he may have been privy to the proposals in the Conservative Education Bill of 1868 to give grants to secular schools, but he used the argument that as grants under the

Revised Code were based on success in an examination in secular subjects only, the voluntary subscriptions were more than enough to pay for the religious teaching given. He used the same argument to explain his support for the Education Bill of 1870. Despite the smallness of the Voluntaryist party, it caused a considerable amount of irritation, perhaps more than the High Church party, because it divided the Nonconformists and made it difficult to reach a national policy. The High Churchmen, on the other hand, remained within the National Society and tried to control its policy. Both Miall, and more particularly Baines, must be blamed for exploiting religious feeling for their own personal prestige.

The religious parties and the state

The association of education with religious teaching dates from the foundation of the Christian Church in England. If the parson could not undertake all the education that was necessary, then the teachers were his assistants, acting as a kind of subordinate clergy. There was no serious likelihood in England that the idea of state education would spring from an opposition to all religious training, as in France. The state, therefore, had to work with the religious groups which controlled the existing schools and try to improve them. The money which came from private sources was never a reliable and regular sum and it was not possible to ensure that schools once built would have a regular income, so that they could continue with efficiency. The state not only provided some of the money, but in the long run it had to provide the legal authority to ensure that children went to school. The attempt to encourage school attendance by statutes limiting the employment of children did not in the end prove adequate.

The great majority of Churchmen and dissenters were prepared to accept Government aid and in the main welcomed the visits of the Inspectors who had been appointed by the Committee of Privy Council after 1839. It was many months before agreement was reached with the religious groups on the appointment of these Inspectors, but as inspection became a condition of the grants they were accepted by the schools so long as the respective Churches had some say in the appointments. The original grants had been paid to the National Society and the British and Foreign School Society, but after the Inspectors were appointed the grants were paid to the managers of the schools who were thus made responsible. To ensure that the money was properly spent, Lord John Russell's government of

1847 introduced a Minute making specific management clauses compulsory. In this way it was hoped to ensure that building grants were not paid for schools which never came to life. The management clauses in the trust deeds of the schools were also intended to ensure that parents in the area would support the school, which was important in small communities comprising persons of several religious denominations. There were several forms of management clauses and the trustees had some latitude in choosing the one they would accept for incorporation in their trust deeds.

In the main these clauses were intended to strengthen the authority of the lay managers, because it had been the common practice in Church of England schools to leave all questions of dispute to be settled by the clergyman and the bishop. This gave no satisfaction to the dissenters or even active laymen in the Church, and if there were a serious disagreement it was likely that the contributions from lay sources would decline. Lay managers could also play an important part in persuading parents to send their children to the school, particularly when the parents were employees of a school manager. The problem had been discussed during the Conservative administration of Peel, but no firm action was taken. The Whig Government of 1846–52 insisted on the recognition of these clauses. A precaution had been taken to win the support of the National Society, but it only gave lukewarm approval by promising to recommend the clauses.

The Times in April 1848 published two letters, one signed 'Clericus' and the other 'Anglicanus', which asserted that the acceptance of the Management Clauses would mean the triumph of the state over Church education. The Committee of Council, it was said, without any legislative powers was trying to enforce a compulsory system by its Minutes. Considerable feeling was shown at the annual meeting of the National Society in June 1848, when the Bishop of Oxford said: 'Perish all state assistance, if the education given by it was the mere stuffing the heads of children with secular education instead of training them up in the nurture of the Christian Church.'[13] It seemed as if the National Society would withdraw completely from participation in the Government grants, but in the end this issue was left undecided. A no-compromise party of High Churchmen was formed under the leadership of Archdeacon Denison, but there was no complete breakaway.

In 1850 the subject was again discussed in Parliament and the Conservatives supported the protesting clergy. The Whig Government was not in the mood to grant any concessions, particularly when extravagant language was used. 'We observe', said a petition quoted in the House in a debate in July 1850, 'that this Committee [of Privy Council] does not recognise the Church as the teacher of the people, but regards various and conflicting religionists as equally qualified to teach, and thus is morally disqualified from exercising any influence over the form and substance of religious instruction'.[14]

There was a stormy meeting of the National Society in June 1851, but moderate views prevailed and even *The Times* warned the High Church faction about bringing the Church into contempt. The Conservative Government of 1852 modified the Minute of 1847 so that the schoolmaster was placed under the control of the ecclesiastical authorities if his teaching should be defective on either religious or moral grounds, and at the same time the position of the lay managers was weakened. A story was told in the House of a 'master, after having been charged with misconduct and proved to have appeared in school in a state of intoxication and to have made use of blasphemous language, had been continued in the school, because when the case was submitted to the committee of the school, who were farmers in the parish, it was found he had nine children, and that if he was removed the expense of their maintenance would fall upon the rates, and they would have to support them'.[15] Gladstone, despite his High Church tendencies, supported the Whig policy and he said in a debate in June 1852, 'nothing is so important as to introduce a great deal of lay agency, both as regards schools and ecclesiastical concerns; but in the schools it is particularly necessary'.

The following year Lord John Russell was again in office and the Conservative Minutes was suspended and the authority of the lay managers was again increased. The matter attracted very little notice and caused no more dissension. It should not be forgotten that the Management Clauses applied equally to the dissenters.

There was less trouble in the years that followed, until 1861 when the Revised Code, and later the Conscience Clause, roused strong objections. All local managers objected to the new system of grants on examination results as determined by the Revised Code and the Committee of Privy Council was again denounced for legislating by Minute. The Code was particularly condemned for its secularising tendency, because grants were awarded for success in the three Rs, but not for the fourth R—religious knowledge. The Committee defended its policy by pointing out that the grants were reduced if religious teaching was found to be unsatisfactory. In most cases the Inspectors themselves were members of the same religious body as the schools under their care.

The Conscience Clause was responsible for as much bitterness as the Revised Code. It had been under consideration from 1853 but it was not insisted on till 1861 when it was found that attempts at conciliation to protect religious minorities were not entirely successful. It was only made a requirement where the school served a mixed religious population and a building grant was not forthcoming if the Clause were refused. The dispute was intimately concerned with the Education Act of 1870 and the details will be considered later. It was, however, another battlefield in which the High Churchmen enjoyed themselves.

Thus the state in most of its attempts to secure educational efficiency was opposed by one or other religious body or subordinate religious group. The Church accepted educational grants but was unwilling to concede any of its authority in return for them. The state after a struggle secured the right to inspect schools and to make Trust Deeds conform to certain standards. By insisting on the employment of certificated teachers, by regulating the ventilation and sanitation of schools, by giving grants for books and apparatus, for the regular attendance of scholars and for pupil teachers, the standard of education slowly improved. But at every step the Voluntary Societies were strengthened in their control over the educational system. The larger annual grants enabled them to keep up their schools and as annual grants increased, more voluntary aid was given to build new schools. Founders of schools need not leave a large endowment because annual grants could be relied on, at least until the Revised Code led to some drastic reductions in 1862. By 1870 a dual system of schools was inevitable—the new ones provided out of the rates where there were not enough school places and the others built and supported by religious bodies. The voluntary system was justified in the minds of its supporters by the religious character of the education given and also because it provided a bond between the various ranks of society. The parson, the philanthropists, the parents and the children were thus drawn together, and some thought that this explained in part the failure of revolutionary movements in England at a time when Europe was very unsettled.

Any extension of the state authority was opposed to the current ideas of *laissez-faire*. If the results were obtainable with a minimum of interference and cost, then it was preferable to leave the work of education to the religious bodies. No concessions were made to those who wished to get aid for secular schools, and even Ragged Schools, obtained very skimpy help, because they were not for the respectable poor who paid a few pence each week for their children's schooling.

In 1862 Lowe, as Vice-President of the Committee of Privy Council, said in Parliament that his department was impartial among the sects, and he was promptly attacked for referring to the Church of England as a sect.

The sects were guilty of taking too narrow a view of education. There were even biblical arithmetics and geographies. One M.P. quoted a sample: 'There were twelve apostles, twelve patriarchs and four evangelists; multiply the patriarchs and apostles together and divide by the evangelists. Solomon had so many hundred wives and so many hundred concubines; subtract the concubines from the wives or the wives from the concubines—I forget which for I have not mastered the niceties of the subject' was his conclusion. One school book of this kind was written by the Secretary of the National Society.

The Church gained more financial aid from the state because it was the largest religious body with the support of the wealthiest people in the country, and also it had a long historical tradition of working with the state. Some dissenters would have preferred Disestablishment and worked to that end, but even the Roman Catholic Earl of Arundel and Surrey thought that the established Church must be predominant. Indeed *The Times* in May 1843 said: 'The Church is the main element of stability in the constitution of the country; she is always on the side of the law; while her enemies of every kind, whether Dissenting, Romish or infidel, have all their alliances with the movements which tend to disorganise society.'[16]

The Nonconformists gained their successes by struggling against the Established Church. They were not accustomed to working in conjunction with the state and had no financial relationship to it. It was only through the state, however, that they had achieved the removal of some of their religious disabilities, though they were to find that a change in the law did not always bring about a change in opinion, even as coloured voters in the Southern States of the U.S.A. find that opinion is lagging behind the law. The legal advantages they had secured led them to hope for further improvements even to the extent of the disestablishment of the Church of England. These optimistic views were severely shattered when the Factory Bill of 1843 was introduced into the House and Hume said in the debate on 24 March 1843, that the Bill was an attempt 'to restore to the Church that power which it formerly possessed'. Two months later while the Bill was still being debated, Ewart said that he must strenuously oppose it 'as a measure adverse to religious freedom'.

When the Minutes of 1846 were introduced, the Nonconformists argued that the Church would get the most benefit and thought that safeguards should be introduced so that public money was spent undenominationally. The Committee of Privy Council, however, pursued an impartial policy but the greater wealth of the Church and the uncooperative attitude of some Nonconformists made it unrealistic to expect any other result. This led the Nonconformists to favour unsectarian and secular schemes of education when they were introduced into Parliament, more especially as they feared another Bill such as that of 1843. When the Bill of 1870 showed that even a Liberal Government would not reduce the financial advantages of the Church, they were indeed offended and the election of 1874 at which Gladstone was defeated was in part due to the opposition of the Nonconformists.

A few Churchmen and a larger number of Nonconformists were keen Secularists. They agreed with the Newcastle Commission when it said: 'There is no doubt that the managers, whether members of the Church of England or Dissenters, attach a great importance to the education of the children over whose parents they have influence, in the religious creeds they themselves profess; but this feeling does not appear to exist in such strength in the parents themselves.'[17] The indifference of parents was proof to the Secularists that the day schools were not the proper place for religious education. The Archbishop of York took the opposite view, and at the annual meeting of the National Society in 1861 said: 'There was, however, still a great want felt of what was generally called distinctive religious education, because the Bible being read in schools of the British and Foreign School Society, it was interpreted in such a manner as to offend the prejudices and prepossessions of no religious sect or denomination. The Church of England, therefore, could not rest satisfied under such a state of things.'[18] Should such a faith offend? There is no doubt that the Church of England more particularly used its powerful position to use methods of proselytism, though it would be impossible to say how successful they were. This added to the bitterness of the Nonconformists.

The Roman Catholics found it even more difficult than the Nonconformists to educate their children. They attached even more importance to dogmatic religious teaching than the Churchmen. A Roman Catholic Inspector of Schools reported in 1860 that some Protestant mill owners enforced the half-time attendance of their child employees in their own Protestant mill schools. 'Many Catholic children, thus compelled to attend, abstain from learning anything for fear of learning that which is objectionable.' Some such employers were content to exact the school pence while allowing the children to attend Catholic schools, but as this meant that the school fee had to be paid twice not many parents could afford this luxury. If the child did not pay his school pence to the employer then he was dismissed. Such cases were the subject of reports in the Parliamentary Papers in the years 1856 to 1860. The most serious disadvantage of the Catholics was the lack of wealthy supporters and the poverty of the parents, often Irish immigrants who could not pay the fees, so that the schools could not qualify for the Government grants.

Thus, despite the impartiality of the state, the opposing religious sects made it impossible to develop a national system which would provide for all children. The intolerant and extravagant language of the High Churchmen and the Voluntaryists made reconciliation impossible. Our Victorian ancestors were of course convinced of the reality of Hell and therefore only a religious education would suffice. Dependence on Sunday Schools only for such religious education seems to us an obvious solution but the Church already controlled many day schools and it would be unreasonable to expect it to give up its hold on education. Many of the parsons did excellent work and gave freely of their own time and money to help the schools. As the business man added to his store of capital, so it was the duty of the priest, the parson and the minister to do what he could to build up his flock.

While the parson can be excused for the part he played, the same cannot be said of the Church. The archbishops and bishops played no dignified part which is worthy of remembrance. They were more inclined to support the view of the dogmatic Archdeacon Denison than the moderate views of Charles Kingsley, Frederick Maurice and Dr Hook, the Vicar of Leeds. The Church of England, just because it made a parade of its superior position, should have been the first to show a more forward outlook, though no human society can be blamed for not having the foresight to see beyond its generation.

It is curious to note that the Radicals implicitly believed that the education of the masses would strengthen the cause of Radicalism. Yet in England parsons formed the largest body of educated men and parsons were the strongest opponents of Radicalism. On the other hand, parsons had little faith in the education of the masses, though they valued it for their own children and for themselves. Both parsons and Radicals were right, but it is not so much their views of education as their views of society which caused the difference of outlook and therefore the relation of education and social opinion must now be considered.

REFERENCES

1. *The Times*, 12 Oct. 1860.
2. Hans. 17 July 1846, vol. 87, c. 1254.
3. Hans. 22 May 1851, vol. 116, c. 1251–2.
4. PP 1860, vol. 54, p. 221.
5. Hans. 15 Mar. 1870, vol. 199, c. 1987, Lord Robert Montagu.
6. Hans. 24 Mar. 1843, vol. 67, c. 1445.
7. TNAPSS, 1867, pp. 99–100, T. Andrews quoting the Archdeacon.
8. *The Times*, 12 Nov. 1866, letter. On 24 Nov. 1866, the editor referred to the assumption and impertinence of this letter.
9. Crosby Hall Lectures 1848, Lect. 7, p. 232; Lect. 3, p. 86.
10. Hans. 12 June 1856, vol. 142, c. 1362. Barnes was a Voluntaryist.
11. Crosby Hall Lectures 1848, Lect. 3, p. 77.
12. Hans. 12 June 1856, vol. 142, c. 1360.
13. *The Times*, 8 June 1848.
14. Hans. 4 July 1850, vol. 112, c. 939.
15. Hans. 21 June 1852, vol. 122, c. 1111.
16. *The Times*, leader, 26 May 1843. See also 17 June 1843: 'those engaged in Dissenting establishments embarked in shoals in the disturbances of last year'.
17. PP 1861, vol. 21, part 1, p. 34.
18. *The Times*, 7 June 1861.

4

The Social Problem of Education

Religious opinion was the most important factor in encouraging the development of education in the building of schools and in the supply of training colleges for teachers. Whether in the early stages the state would have done the work better without the religious bodies is extremely doubtful. In any case the ruling classes, particularly in Parliament, were mostly adherents of some religious body and, therefore, they were not likely to involve the state in measures which would be opposed by all churches. Until 1870 the Committee of Privy Council maintained its rule that grants would not be given to secular schools.

The building of schools tended to create an educational demand, but the ordinary working-class parent and the average employer were not so much influenced by religious views. The demand for child labour was often deplored but almost as often regarded as inevitable and neither priest nor minister was prepared to emphasise the superior necessity of education itself. They accepted the current social and economic theories and prophesied that education would unfit the labourer for his work, or, with the fifth commandment in mind, said it was the duty of the child to help his parents. Church of England parsons were, on the whole, conservative, and as the country clerics had an undue influence in the Church, so the problems of the towns were underestimated.

In the present generation we are again beginning to realise the unpopularity of local rates as a form of general taxation. This feeling was particularly strong in the nineteenth century because the high rates of the Napoleonic War period had made landowners afraid of any return to conditions which had existed before the reform of the Poor Law in 1834. Many Radicals in asking for support for their schemes of rate-provided schools failed to realise how far this prejudice against rates persisted. The Radicals in general were not members of the landowning class and it was the landowners who voiced the strongest feelings against any increase in the rates. The alternative of income tax was not regarded any more favourably. This tax, which had been levied to help defeat the French, was so much disliked that when it was withdrawn in 1815, Parliament ordered that all documents about the tax should be destroyed. Sir Robert Peel reintroduced income tax in 1842 as a temporary measure until the loss of income from lower import duties should be restored by the growing trade which it was expected would follow in a few years. In fact the tax has been continued ever since, despite the occasional promises of Gladstone to abolish it. As there was no other important source of income at that time the state had to rely on help from philanthropists to build schools and fees from parents to maintain them, so that state grants could be kept to a minimum.

The resources of philanthropy, though practically unlimited in those times of low taxation, could not be relied on. The uncertainty of income from local contributors was one of the main problems of school managers. The death of a wealthy subscriber, his removal from the district or a local quarrel might be the ruin of a good school. The payment by the state of building grants and annual grants relieved the school managers of much financial worry, but nevertheless they could not manage without school fees which in any case were made necessary by the Minutes of the Privy Council.

It was taken for granted that parents would pay for the education of their children, if only a penny a week, and this principle was preserved in the Education Act of 1870. Even a penny a week for each child was a considerable sum to a country labourer earning ten shillings a week or less, though reductions were usually made when there were many children from one family. There were other expenses too, for children could hardly attend school badly dressed (at least not until schooling was compulsory) because mothers were often too respectable to let this happen. With older children there could be other expenses too, perhaps books or a weekly sum towards the school treat. The parents must also have considered the possible financial gain of sending the child to work, though it is reported by one Inspector in 1867 that 'Essex and Suffolk children's earnings do their parents very little good, for when the extra food and clothing required are taken into consideration there is little, if any, profit gained by their labour'.

There were some broad differences between the problems of education in agricultural and industrial areas and between schools for the poor and schools for paupers and these will now be separately considered.

Education in the towns

The growth of towns in the nineteenth century showed up the gaps in the educational system. Because of the larger numbers it became possible to provide schools for all denominations, instead of one parish school, which was often a source of sectarian trouble. In the towns it was also possible to build larger, better and cheaper schools than the small villages could provide. On the other hand, trade prosperity one year and trade depression the next affected the town schools more seriously and made the teachers' task more difficult. Trade prosperity sometimes had an adverse effect on school attendance, while hard times led many parents to ask for remission of fees. 'In all towns masters and mistresses of the day schools asserted that if trade were good, in less than a fortnight the children would leave', said one official in 1843. But while poorer children were drawn away from school in prosperous times—'the more employment for the hands, the less instruction for the head', as one Inspector put it— the better artisans increased their expenditure on the education of their children. Consequently there were fewer places for poor children and the schools tended to go up in social grade, so that teachers did not want the poor children back. One who attended regularly earned more Government grant and was a better pupil than the casual attender.

The improvement of trade after the depression of 1857 caused school attendance to diminish, but the distress in Lancashire during the American Civil War of 1861–5 which cut off supplies of cotton, led to a better attendance but also to a loss of income from fees and less financial help from voluntary subscribers. Local fluctuations of trade and prosperity also caused families to move around, so that children had to change from one school to another, which was no benefit either to pupil or teacher, particularly as the period of school life was so short. One Inspector noted the compensating advantage in good times of a larger attendance at the factory school, but the education there was generally of a poor standard.

In 1841 wool weaving was generally carried out by hand and there were also many hand loom weavers in the cotton industry. In the engineering industries power machinery came much later. Employment at home in such handicrafts, or in the fields, was often considered an education in itself and was generally accepted as a necessity. Working conditions in the towns and the growth of the factory system influenced the expansion of education. If mother went out to work, she wanted some older child or children to look after the home and babies and her absence also made it easier for some youngsters to play truant from school. One of the objects of the National Association for the Promotion of Social Science, an important body founded in 1857, was to encourage the 'extension of the industrial employment of women and of their better education for that end'.

The factories offered profitable employment for children and some chose the factory in place of the school room. Disraeli, in his novel *Sybil*, and also some Inspectors of schools in their reports of 1847 and 1848, referred to the use of machinery in various occupations whereby 'the labour of young children is made more valuable than it ever was before, so that, instead of the parent supporting the child, the reverse is often the case'.[1] But there is no doubt that far more children were employed at home or in unregulated industries than in factories subject to legislative control, and they may well have worked under very bad conditions. Children in the better factories, at any rate, worked more regular hours and in some cases they had legal protection, for what it was worth.

Faced with these difficulties, what were the remedies proposed by the educationists of the period? The Newcastle Commission in its report of 1861 opposed the idea of compulsory education but saw no objection to 'private compulsion exercised by employers on their workmen as to the education of their children. As the relation between employers and workmen is one of contract, there can be no objection to the introduction of any terms into it to which both sides consent.'[2] They reported favourably on the educational scheme of the Lead (London) Company at Middleton. Boys had to attend school from six to twelve years and girls from six to fourteen. 'Boys of twelve are available for lead washing, and may be supposed to have gained as much literary instruction at twelve as the girls at fourteen, because much of the girls' school time is occupied with needlework.' It is, of course, more than likely that the girls were of no use to a lead company as cheap labour. Sir Stafford Northcote, well known for his part authorship of the report on the reform of the Civil Service, said in Parliament in July 1860: 'The relation between parent and child was one with which the state had no right to interfere, but the relation between the employer and the child was a public relation, by means of which the parent might be stimulated to do his duty.'[3] The idea was very favourably received, but there is no evidence that it was widely adopted in practice.

Another suggestion was the use of an educational test before a child was allowed to work. John Stuart Mill had a similar idea as a test to qualify for the vote, and one Radical, Joseph Hume, in 1843 even put it forward as an essential qualification for marriage. Bills were introduced into Parliament in the sessions of 1857–8 and 1860 to prevent the employment of children under the age of sixteen (and, in the 1860 Bill, under twelve) who could not produce an educational certificate or were not attending school part time. These Bills did not become law, but an Act of 1860 forbade the employment of boys under twelve in the mines, except those between ten and twelve who had an educational certificate. These ideas reflect the conflict between the landowners and the factory owners, the former being only too glad to impose a burden on the latter. One Inspector, in his report of 1861, condemned this policy of an educational minimum: 'If a boy could have at ten all that another knows at thirteen, it does not follow that he is equally fit to leave school. He needs the discipline of the school—his real education—as much as the veriest dunce in the class'4—a penetrating observation well in advance of the time. Even W. E. Forster in 1875 proposed compulsory education to nine or ten, when the clever ones could leave, while the dull ones continued with part-time education to thirteen or fourteen; no vision here of an educational ladder for bright children.

Both these ideas of using a clause in the contract between employer and employee and the use of an educational test fitted in with current notions of freedom and free will. Religious freedom, political liberty and the unrestricted right of the parent over his child were more important than legislation to protect the rights of the child. The inconsistency was aptly described by Mr Henley in a parliamentary debate on 17 July 1860: 'What could be more compulsory than to pass a law declaring that those who did not acquire an education should not work and consequently should not eat.'

A partial recognition of the need to protect pauper children appeared in the first Factory Act of 1802. But the educational clauses, which were first introduced in the Act of 1833, were a mixed blessing. Firstly, they tended to make the regulated employments unattractive to employers, parents and children. If the labour could be found elsewhere at no greater cost, then the employer would do without the children. If the parent or child found that the earnings were greater in the unregulated trades, then they preferred them. It was observed everywhere that the Acts caused children to leave the regulated factories so that they found themselves in conditions which most likely were worse than before, but statistics show that the total number in the regulated occupations was steadily rising throughout the period to 1870. Secondly, the schools formed under the Factory Acts were usually unsatisfactory. Few schoolmasters were properly qualified, the buildings were often poor and the Factory Inspectors had no adequate powers to control schools to make certain that the teaching was effective. It was not uncommon, however, for factory children to attend grant-aided schools under the Committee of Privy Council. Here they were a disruptive element among children who attended full-time; some attended in the mornings and some in the afternoons; not many factory workers' offspring were likely to be as clean or as well-behaved as the full-timers; indeed, the efforts of the teachers to interest the half-timers when they were tired out and to keep them abreast of the work of other children must have proved almost fruitless. *The Times* reported in 1868 that a Wesleyan school in Bolton had turned away all the half-time pupils because of their low grant-earning capacity, the difficulty of educating them and the objection to mixing ragamuffins with genteel children. One side effect was noted by the Newcastle Commission, namely that children intended for the factories had rarely attended infant schools, as the parents would not send them when compulsory education was inevitable later on. These young ignoramuses also produced another awkward problem for the teacher. The Factory Acts were extended in 1864 and 1867 to other industries, and educational clauses were included, but they were not considered a success; they showed up educational deficiences and thus convinced some people of the need for a national system of education, while others thought that it would be enough to strengthen the education clauses of the Factory Acts.

There were, of course, those who thought differently, and in 1860 one Factory Inspector is quoted in *The Times* as saying: 'I am persuaded that in no way can the children of the operative classes be placed in more favourable circumstances than while working in a well regulated factory under the conditions of the existing law. Their half day's employment can do no injury to their health, they are exposed to no undue exertions, and they are sheltered from the weather in a dry and warm room—a great contrast to what most of them would otherwise be exposed to; if the school to which they are sent daily for three hours be a reasonably good one, they get the advantage of some education and in many of the schools they obtain the lasting benefit of most effective teaching. When they are in the mill they acquire regular and industrious habits and by the work they are set to do and by what they see around them, their wits are sharpened and they earn wages that must go a good way towards their maintenance.'[5] This view was supported by Edwin Chadwick, the well-known and well-hated former Poor Law Commissioner, who in 1862 thought that the Factory Acts protected children from overwork in both factories and schools. He emphasised the evil of sedentary education and the value of military drill. Yet factory schools, even if universal, would not have been any use to children under the statutory age of employment. In 1868 it was estimated that less than 80,000 children were receiving compulsory education under the Factory Acts.

The provision of infant schools and evening schools was also proposed as a remedy for failing to educate children of normal school age. One Inspector suggested that all young persons under the Factory Acts between thirteen and eighteen should be compelled to attend evening schools; but he had little support for his idea. The Newcastle Commission recommended infant schools for children aged three to seven and the government grants under the Revised Code of 1862 offered favourable terms for children under six. The idea of part-time education for teenagers has persisted; it was a remedy put forward in the Act of 1918, which abolished half-time education under the Factory Acts, but the 'day continuation schools' were an unfulfilled dream. The Education Act of 1944 also promised county colleges with the same object in view, but they too have been one of the many schemes which have gone astray. As for nursery schools, the effects of two wars, the shortage of teachers and of classrooms have meant that Public Health authorities have invaded this field, in order to care for children while their mothers are at work, and the educational aspects have been of secondary importance.

All these remedies were doomed to failure because public opinion was not ripe for change and the various governments were not prepared to give a lead. Employers did not approve of a national system of education. An Inspector of Nonconformist schools in the northern counties reported in 1852 that 'the employer stands, as it were, in antagonism to the teacher, regarding him as one of the agents in carrying out and enforcing a hostile Act of Parliament, which it is his interest, if not to thwart, at least to reduce to the smallest amount of practical effect. The child is accordingly screened from blame in giving way either to irregular or unpunctual attendance.'[6] Edward Baines, a determined opponent of state education on religious grounds, was a strong supporter of *laissez-faire*; he said in a letter to *The Times* in April 1856, that as the employer paid the just wages of his child employees according to the law of supply and demand, to force him to pay for their education as well was to make charity compulsory, and this was not in accordance with English liberty. In Parliament both Lord John Russell in March 1856 and the Earl of Harrowby in July 1854 protested against the indifference, and sometimes the active opposition, of employers to part-time education. In 1860 a paper was read at the general meeting of the National Society for the Promotion of Social Science 'On the inexpediency of compelling employers to educate their work children', and in 1865 at a similar meeting a speaker argued against the extension of the Factory Acts to the Sheffield trades.

It was generally felt that the rights of parents over their children should not be violated and the industry of the child was regarded as essential to family life, as it was necessary for industrial prosperity. Sir James Kay-Shuttleworth protested in 1857 against the argument that England's commercial pre-eminence was dependent on cheap labour and that education must be subservient to its demands. Yet W. Cowper, when he was the political head of the Education Department, said in 1858: 'So urgent and permanent were the demands for children's labour, that he despaired of seeing any measure adopted that would induce the working classes to keep their children at school long enough to acquire a complete education.'[7] The Registrar of the Newcastle Commission considered that 'labour of all kinds requires a long apprenticeship in itself, if the young are to be worth anything at all in the labour market'.

It is difficult to estimate how far parents desired the education of their children. Considering the increasing number of children at school, it might be thought that parents were demanding more and more education, but attendance was irregular and the number on the roll was certainly inflated because there was reluctance to remove a name from the register. Sometimes attendance was probably due to pressure from the parson, the squire or some local philanthropist, rather than to parental enthusiasm. The certifying surgeons who examined children before they were admitted to factory work found they had to reject some applications because children were under age, underdeveloped or diseased; this shows there was no desire for education on the part of some parents. On the other hand, in some places workmen arranged for their masters to deduct school fees from their wages. But in 1860 an Inspector for the north of England reported that despite considerable interest taken by parents in the education of their children, there was 'amongst a considerable class of the working population, a deficiency in the demand for education, and a reluctancy to make full use of the supply actually offered'.[8] It would be unreasonable to expect that uneducated parents would place a high value on education, particularly when the family income was so low and the fear of the Poor Law all pervading. Even in the 1930s some children in grammar schools who had won scholarships or free places were taken away from school soon after they had passed the compulsory age of fourteen-plus, despite the fact that there was a moral obligation on them to keep the child at school to sixteen, and sometimes a legal obligation too, which was rarely enforced.

The towns highlighted the problem of education and the social conditions made it more urgent to find some answer to the serious difficulties and dangers which beset children. In rural areas the changes were not so significant and the parson and the squire could help to solve the difficulties; but there was not the same background of social cohesion in the towns, though not all employers were indifferent to the schools and not all workmen were educational enthusiasts, as some would have us think.

Education in rural areas

The transition from the eighteenth to the nineteenth century in rural areas was not so marked as in the towns. There had been village schools before the education of the masses was conceived as a social duty. Since most of the village schools were under the Church of England they had been stimulated by the National Society and its development of the monitorial teaching method, which was later replaced by the pupil teacher system. In Parliament the manufacturers sometimes taunted the landowners on the subject of child labour in their own self defence; for instance, one M.P. said, in March 1856: 'In some agricultural districts in the north of England the children went out as early as six years of age to tend sheep and cattle. He would commend that fact to Gentlemen on the opposite side who were so anxious about factory inspection.' When Lord Ashley (later the Earl of Shaftesbury) introduced the educational debates of February 1843, Lord John Russell remarked that there was as great ignorance in rural districts as in the manufacturing districts to which Lord Ashley particularly referred. A writer in *The Times* of 24 October 1864 defended the landowners by saying that education was more necessary in the towns because it would reduce strikes and the influence of demagogues. As late as 1866 Lord Shaftesbury protested against the illogical and cruel suggestion that nothing should be done for factory children because the education of children in rural areas was defective. He realised that country children could not be taught by the half-time system, but suggested school on alternate days.

The average squire and farmer cared little for the parish school and the parson bore the brunt of the work of supporting it, often from his own pocket. An Inspector reported in 1845 that the educated classes hold the 'notion that the cultivation of the intellect unfits for manual labour', and they were afraid 'that education may destroy the present relations between master and servant and substitute no better. That instead of a plodding, hard-working peasantry, who do their labour much as the animals they tend, we shall have an effeminate class of persons, averse to rough work, conceited and insubordinate.'⁹ Charles Kingsley, as a country parson, knew his squirearchy. The bluff squire in his novel *Yeast* advised the earnest young man to stick to fox hunting and not to turn the heads of the poor with 'cursed education'. The squire's gentle daughter was 'a staunch believer in that peculiar creed which allows everyone to feel for the poor except themselves'. The local lord, who was a serious young Conservative philanthropist, was described as one who 'fats prize labourers, just as Lord M. fats prize oxen and pigs'.

The diocesan Inspectors of schools even reported some clergy as being opposed to state intervention in their schools. Some of them, it was said in 1858, 'deem the mechanical art of reading and writing, the text of the Church catechism and Mrs Trimmer, to be the aim of all education for the labouring classes, and conceive that the development of the intellect which God gave to man for culture would tend to revolutionise society and unfit the poor man for his station in life'. Education had 'spoilt the race of domestic servants'—an objection as old as Aristophanes—and taught them to write love letters.

Among farmers it was often a condition of the employment of the parent that his children were available to give help when necessary, and if the children were kept at school, the father was threatened with dismissal. Lord John Russell said in 1856 he had heard of a farmer who 'would not give anything to a day school, because he finds that since a Sunday school had been established the birds have increased and eaten his corn, and because he cannot now procure the services of the boys whom he used to employ the whole of Sunday in protecting his fields'.¹⁰

The farmers agreed with the M.P. who said in the same debate: 'If children were to be kept at school till they were fifteen years old, how were they to obtain a knowledge of farming or become skilful farm servants?' These opinions were based on the facts of child labour, for it was quite usual for children between six and eight years of age to be kept in the fields for seven days a week to scare away the crows, and older children were often at work on the farm for four months of the year. One Inspector reported that a child of eleven was earning six shillings a week and this was more than the sum paid to pupil teachers, who received £10 to £20 per annum from age thirteen to eighteen years. *The Times* in 1867 thought that the low earnings of the farm worker were such that a boy must go to field work as soon as he is physically equal to it, and he often does go earlier.

The work of the rural school teacher was made very difficult with so much absenteeism. One of the government grants introduced in 1853 specifically to help rural schools was calculated on a basis of forty-eight weeks' attendance in the year, and the Bishop of Salisbury pointed out that in his rural parishes it was impossible to satisfy such a condition. It was also noted by an Inspector in 1857 that 'children of labourers rarely continue in the school longer than three years, and many not longer than one year. The parents are usually engaged by the year, and often leave the neighbourhood at the expiration of that time.' Martinmas was still the recognised changing day for farm servants, and in the 1850s the date of the old-style calendar was still observed in some places.

The village school was also troubled by class consciousness. One Inspector found that 'attempts to unite in education the children of the agricultural labourer with the children of the employer of labour will not succeed in consequence of the feeling of the upper class against such a union'. Agricultural improvements of the nineteenth century were also said to lead to the employment of younger children, particularly the new turnip and mangel cutting methods; not that all farmers were well advanced, for it was found that a Reformatory School in Norfolk was still, in 1857, teaching boys to leave half the land fallow.

There is little evidence of the opinions of the agricultural labourers on these matters, because they were illiterate; but Charles Kingsley was probably well acquainted with them and he puts these words into the mouth of one of his characters: 'Why, when I was a boy, we never had no schooling. And now mine goes and learns singing and jobrafy and ciphering and sich like. Not that I sees no good in it. We was a sight better off in the old times, when there weren't no schooling. Schooling harn't made wages rise, nor preaching neither.'[11] The backwardness of the country school seems all the more surprising when it is realised that between 1850 and 1875 times were good for farmers and landowners. The profit was there, but not much of it went to the schools.

Education and social status

The educational opinions in agricultural and industrial areas had much in common. The majority of employers were opposed to the education of the poor and this was due as much to preconceived social ideas as to the supposed necessity for child labour. Education was associated with the idea of class distinction and the quality and quantity of education required for the children of one class was considered to be a separate problem from that required for those cf another class of society. Within limits such an idea was true, but it was not realised that any limits existed. From the provision of schools for pauper and criminal children to the growing demand for middle-class education, there was a carefully graded scheme by which one class was separated from another. Some exceptional men looked forward to a truly national system of education but these enthusiasts were ignored by the practical politicians.

Many educational reformers hoped that the education of paupers and criminals would cure them of their crime and pauperism. This expectation applied also to those who, if steps were not taken, might become criminals and paupers. Lord John Russell in his letter to the Queen in 1839 urging the appointment of a Privy Council Committee on Education argued that the community would benefit from the education of pauper children, orphans and the children of criminals. Spencer Walpole agreed with the opinion in the Poor Law report of 1834 that one fault of the old poor laws was the principle that 'the children shall not suffer for the misconduct of their parents'. The Ven. Archdeacon Allen at the Social Science Association meeting in 1858 was a little more sympathetic. 'Unhappily children must suffer for the misdeeds of their parents, we cannot help those who will not help themselves'.

The education of pauper children was the most pressing problem and they had to be separated 'from the intercourse with the depraved inmates' of the workhouses. Every effort was made to persuade the Guardians of adjoining areas to cooperate and provide one district school separate from the workhouses. Despite the work of Kay-Shuttleworth, who had been a Poor Law Inspector, only a few Guardians followed this policy, but in some places they sent the children to the ordinary schools of the parish. One Inspector found the experiment successful; 'The parents of higher grade very soon become reconciled to their attendance, and the children generally admit them into their society without difficulty or reflection upon their social inferiority.' This was in 1856, but three years later another

5

Inspector said: 'The system of sending pauper children to outdoor schools works as ill as ever. The children learn next to nothing, fail to be blended with those of independent labourers, and lose all the benefit of that continuous training and industrial discipline which a teacher in a workhouse school can alone administer.'[12]

Industrial discipline was an important principle of the workhouse schools. 'One of the first things to be done', said the letter of instructions to Inspectors of 1847, 'is to devise proper employments for the scholars, suited to develop their strength, and to prepare them for a course of honest industry.' Some Guardians were reported in 1859 as so eager for industrial training that they did not leave enough time for ordinary teaching, for which the minimum was supposed to be eighteen hours a week. One of the Assistant Commissioners of the Newcastle Commission thought that 'the education of certain classes might also be compulsory, as of paupers in workhouses, criminals in gaols; but in the latter case it should be confined to moral, religious and industrial, as anything tending to sharpen their wits would probably be productive of greater mischief than ignorance itself'.[13] Perhaps he had some foresight of the Great Train Robbers. It is clear that industrial training was valued because idle hands were considered more dangerous than idle brains and active brains than active hands. It is only too evident from the debates in Parliament that learning itself was distrusted except for the few.

While the education of the children of indoor paupers, including orphans and deserted children, was compulsory, that of children whose parents received outdoor relief was voluntary, and until the passing of Denison's Act in 1855, the Guardians did not have definite authority to provide for their education. An Inspector of schools in 1850 found that in agricultural districts many Boards of Guardians refused outdoor relief to parents who were sending their children to school. Denison's Act was only permissive, but its scope was wide. The Guardians were allowed to help outdoor paupers to pay for the education of their children between four and sixteen at inspected schools, but education was not to be a condition of relief and parents were free to select any aided school. If the Guardians had been zealous educationists this might have provided a basis for a national system of education at a later stage, but the Act was administered in the same spirit as that which inspired the debates in Parliament. 'It was the duty of the poor to educate their children as much as it was to provide them with food; and it would be the duty of the Board (of Guardians) to ascertain that the parents could not pay for their children's education before admitting them'—such was the opinion of Lord Lyttelton, which he voiced in the House in June 1855.[14] In 1866 it was stated that only 7,000 children were being educated under the Act and this was because the Guardians wished to save expenditure; some even refused outdoor relief if children were kept at school. The Newcastle Commission considered that poverty was more often an excuse than a cause of absence of children from school.

The pauper schoolmaster was particularly hampered because children passed out of the workhouse school as soon as the parents became self-supporting. It was only while they were indoor paupers that the children were subject to compulsory attendance and the schoolmaster could not keep the children when the parents were discharged. Orphans and deserted children did of course stay for longer periods but were liable to be moved from one place to another if a contentious Board of Guardians could prove a settlement elsewhere.

Reformatory and industrial schools were owned by Voluntary Societies; the former were for actual criminals and the latter for potential offenders. An Act was passed in 1857 which authorised the magistrates to send young criminals to certified Industrial or Reformatory schools, and as with the Act of 1848 for Poor Law schools the age limit before discharge was high, fifteen for criminals and sixteen for paupers. No doubt the longer school life was thought necessary because of the intractability of the pupils.

There remained the problem of educating the street arabs. These were not considered respectable enough to mix with the children of the 'deserving poor' and in any case their parents were too indifferent to the need for school education. They had of course 'a tolerable prospect of compulsory education, by establishing a claim on the state in the orthodox manner, that is, by getting convicted of crime', or perhaps of pauperism. The Ragged Schools were the only places where such children could be admitted and these schools were not numerous enough to cope with the problem. Not that there was a strong demand for the vacant places; free admission, free meals and occasional gifts of clothing were needed to attract scholars. Some of the most disinterested of philanthropists such as Lord Shaftesbury and Miss Mary Carpenter worked hard for the success of these schools, but it was uphill work.

In 1852 the Government made the first grants to Ragged Schools of 10s per child, and this was considerably increased in 1856. By a Minute of 1857 an attempt was made to force the schools to qualify for the grants under the Industrial Schools Act of that year, but in 1862 the grants under the Minute of 1856 were withdrawn. A Select

Committee had made an investigation in 1861 and Sir Stafford Northcote favoured the continuation of the grants, but the Committee preferred the report of Sir James Graham and the logic of the Liberal carried the day against the sympathies of the Conservative. Grants to Ragged Schools were condemned because either they were sums paid in relief of the poor rates or they competed unfairly with the fee charging schools. Lord Shaftesbury and the Ragged School Union were opposed to any grants because they thought that interest in the schools would decline unless their religious character was maintained and also the appeal to philanthropy would be weakened. The Report also said that 'Infant schools, which take the child before it was contaminated, appear to strike at the root of the evil which Ragged Schools only attack in its more advanced stage'.

The Times, in a sympathetic leading article of 3 December 1853 said: 'From all sides there are accounts of the good effects of infant and ragged schools. It is said that the children exhibit attachment to those who teach them and great powers of acquiring knowledge.' The social conscience, however, put parental responsibility first. Ragged Schools could in theory qualify for grants under the Revised Code, but their standards of education were too low for this to mean anything. The state in demanding guarantees for the efficiency of the schools emphasised the responsibility of parents to pay school fees and to keep their children in regular attendance.

The Radicals were strongly convinced of the need for free schools. Richard Cobden 'believed that when the system of free schools was adopted, such would be the estimation in which education would be held by the mass of the people that it would not be easy to keep children from the schools'. But by 1854, only three years later, he was disillusioned and was very sorry to notice 'that the working people seemed to have a great disinclination to send their children to school'.[15]

The Conservatives took the opposite line; 'To make all schools free would be to stamp pauperism on the whole people, and to produce an evil which would be ten thousand times greater than any advantage to be derived from the possibility of bringing to school the few children whose parents are unable to pay the school pence', so thought J. W. Henley speaking in the House on 2 May 1855. Archdeacon Allen, a former Inspector of schools, writing to *The Times* on 11 October 1858 said: 'Every free school that is established weakens those healthful efforts that are now being made for the improvement of the poor and tends to the demoralisation of parents and the demoralisation of children . . . for what child will be taught gratitude to his parents, or gratitude to his teacher, if he gets his book learning without cost at a state school?' This opinion was endorsed by the Newcastle Commission, which opposed a suggestion that magistrates should have power to order the Guardians to pay the school fees of children of very poor parents.

Those who favoured free education scorned the argument of demoralisation because school pence did not pay more than a third of the total cost of education, but the Newcastle Commission thought that 'if the wages of the child's labour are necessary, either to keep the parents from the poor rates, or to relieve the pressure of severe and bitter poverty, it is far better that it should go to work at the earliest age at which it can bear the physical exertion than that it should remain at school'.[16] Even Sir James Kay-Shuttleworth said at the Social Science meeting of 1860 that 'to protect the child from parental neglect has with us therefore been subordinated to the personal freedom of the parent'.[17]

It was also argued that free education would lead to irregular attendance and that in any case the poor would not appreciate free education because they had found out it was not worth much. 'Many parents regard charity schools as a sort of degradation', partly because the charity of the charitable was sometimes obnoxious and the gift of money was not always made in a charitable spirit. The regulations of the Committee of the Privy Council encouraged a spirit of snobbishness and class consciousness. A school could not qualify for the capitation grants unless the parents paid on an average a sum of not less than 1d nor more than 4d a week, so that provision was limited to the deserving poor; children of the poorest class or of the lower middle class were thus excluded. In the words of the Newcastle Commission, such education was confined to 'the education of the families of day labourers, mechanics, and the poorer classes of farmers and shopkeepers'. In some schools pupils paid the full cost of about 30s per annum, but it was found that in consequence the education of the poorer scholars was neglected.

After the passing of the Revised Code, which modified the rules slightly, there was a slow increase in school fees. Because Government grants declined, it was to the advantage of the school (and of the teacher where the school was farmed out) to admit those children who would attend regularly and whose parents were good payers. This tendency had been noted in the Inspectors' reports as early as 1851. The Inspectors were divided on the policy to be adopted; some favoured a low and uniform fee while others recommended a fee scale adjusted to the means of the parents. One school in Lancashire in 1862 even charged higher fees for education in the higher classes, so that poor children stayed in the lowest class. In fact it was often said that the superior education in the grant-aided schools was drawing pupils from the private schools. The fees which had been 30 per cent of the school income in 1852 had risen to 38 per cent in 1860, and this is not entirely explained by the rise in real wages. In France the fee income was about 25 per cent of the school income.

One individualist remedy for irregular attendance was the introduction of prize schemes to stimulate the interest of parents. They began in 1851 and local philanthropists were canvassed to give the money for cash prizes; it was also expected that children would stay longer at school and that this kind of stimulus was preferable to compulsory education. In fact the prizes often went to children of a higher social class than they were intended for. For some ten years they were fairly popular but Dr Hodgson, one of the officials, said in 1861: 'I will merely say that I am not alone in thinking that such schemes (I speak of prizes much more than of certificates) have in them at least as much danger as advantage. Educational crutches, or go-carts, may for a time sustain the rickety, but they may sustain the rickets too.'

The view was often expressed in Parliament that there was a danger 'of over-educating children, and thereby incapacitating them for those employments which are suited to their station in life'. Robert Lowe in 1862, when defending his Revised Code, said: 'We do not profess to give these children an education that will raise them above their station and business in life.'[18] As early as 1851 Cockburn, a member of the Government of Lord John Russell, said that 'so far from being afraid of instruction, the only question in men's minds was, whether the National Schools were not too highly instructing the people—whether, in regard to the portion of the people who were engaged in outdoor manual occupations, they were not educating them to the prejudice of their physical capacity'.[19] Professor Pillans at the meeting of the National Association for the Promotion of Social Science in 1858 said the working classes could be taught all that was necessary before the age of nine and made practical suggestions for this purpose. Lord Lyveden even saw as the ultimate end of an over-literary education 'the system of the ancient Romans, who gave games to the people for the purpose of amusing them and keeping them quiet'.

Practical education was one of the ideas put forward by the Inspectors, and some argued that the indifference of the parents was due to the scholastic teaching. 'Employers of labour do not value children more for having been at school; and therefore parents do not care to send them', said one Inspector in 1858. In place of practical education it became popular to advocate half time education (see page 48) as the average teacher had no training for practical work. Another sort of practical education was the teaching of economics, which would teach the poor not to join useless strikes, Chartist meetings or similar disturbances. Thus the notion of submission was to be taught both as a religious duty and as an economic necessity. The social slavery imposed by trades unions would be prevented by teaching economics. It was the labourers' ignorance of economic laws which caused machine-breaking, the attempt of trade unions to fix the conditions of work and the evils which followed from driving capital abroad, said Kay-Shuttleworth. The Newcastle Commission displaced cleanliness from its accustomed place when it said: 'Next to religion, the knowledge most important to a labouring man is that of the causes which regulate the amount of his wages, the hours of his work, the regularity of his employment, and the price of what he consumes.'[20] Mr Moses Angel of the Jews Free School went a step further: 'Social economy, properly taught, would give all the religious knowledge they require.' On the other hand: 'I always object', he said in 1861, 'to my pupils playing at marbles, buttons or any game which fosters a spirit of acquisitiveness.'[21]

The social problems of education in the nineteenth century were made more complex by the economic changes and if the ruling class was fairly consistent about the social aims of education, it was not agreed upon the means by which the aims could be achieved. This divergence of view coupled with the disputes on the religious aims of education made governments reluctant to risk their reputations by trying to establish a national system.

REFERENCES

1. PP 1847–8, vol. 50, p. 152.
2. PP 1861, vol. 21, part 1, p. 217.
3. Hans. 17 July 1860, vol. 159, c. 2024.
4. PP 1861, vol. 49, p. 139.
5. *The Times*, 6 June 1860.
6. PP 1852, vol. 40, pp. 565–6.
7. Hans. 11 Feb. 1858, vol. 148, c. 1229.
8. PP 1860, vol. 54, p. 158.
9. PP 1845, vol. 35, p. 102.
10. Hans. 11 Apr. 1856, vol. 141, c. 908.
11. *Alton Locke*, 1850 (1876 edn., p. 133).

12. PP 1859, vol. 21, part 1, p. 522.
13. PP 1861, vol. 21, part 1, p. 198.
14. Hans. 8 June 1855, vol. 138, c. 1646.
15. Hans. 22 May 1851, vol. 116, c. 1287 and 30 June 1854, vol. 134, c. 990.
16. PP 1861, vol. 21, part 1, p. 188.
17. TNAPSS 1860, p. 94.
18. Hans. 13 Feb. 1862, vol. 165, c. 238.
19. Hans. 22 May 1851, vol. 116, c. 1279.
20. PP 1861, vol. 21, part 1, p. 127.
21. PP 1861, vol. 21, part 5, pp. 67 and 46.

5

Schools and Scholars

The growth of the system

The strong feeling against any expansion of the powers of the state in the mid-nineteenth century applied also to the development of education. The policy of the state was to encourage the educational efforts of others and on this basis no system of state education could be built up. While the state shirked its responsibility the religious bodies were incapable of building a nationwide system. The rivalry of the sects and their rivalry with the state did not produce a surplus of schools and cheap education, as some educational 'free-traders' expected, but tended to paralyse the activities of all parties, so that schools were built which could not be maintained and children were taught for such short periods that they could benefit very little from the instruction given.

Yet in the period 1839–70 the state spent over £12·5 million on education and the average attendance of children was over a million by 1870. This was proof enough for the optimists that the grant-aided methods of pre-1870 were satisfactory. Behind the scenes the Committee of Privy Council continued to expand its activities and if its chief officials were not so hated as was Edwin Chadwick they had some of his qualities in magnifying their administrative powers. No one cares about insignificant growths and so the Education Office, after a stormy start, gradually extended its scope until it was found in 1858 that its annual budget exceeded £500,000. It was then too late to unscramble the whole scheme, though the Revised Code was partly directed to this end.

The educational statistics of the period must be treated with considerable caution, but as they were often used to support an argument it is necessary to consider them. Up to 1847 the education grant for any one year had not exceeded £50,000, but by 1853 this had reached £200,000 per annum. The increase was largely due to expenditure on the training of teachers under the Minutes of 1846.

In the years between 1854 and 1858 the grant multiplied by three times as the result of capitation grants, payments to teachers and expenditure on Industrial schools. By 1861 the total was £650,000 per annum, but grants for training colleges were then withdrawn and the next year the Revised Code began to have its effect, so that by 1865 the sum was only £480,000. Changes in Government policy then led to an increase and by 1870 the grant had almost reached £700,000. In relation to the national budget the expenditure from 1840 to 1870 on elementary education had multiplied by ten times.

Increased expenditure by the state was accompanied by greater income from other sources. Thus by 1869, when the national budget for education was £633,000, income from other sources was £925,000, but the greater proportional increase from these other sources since 1862 was largely the result of the Revised Code in reducing the grants. Subscriptions from voluntary sources increased fivefold in the twenty years before 1870 and school fees sevenfold. The increase of fees coupled with the improved average attendance may be partly explained by the transfer of children from private schools to state-aided schools and in part no doubt to the improved economic position of the artisan classes. In 1864 the number of individual voluntary subscribers was about 163,000 and the average subscription of half of them was less than £1 per annum. There were also sums collected through the Church and other general sources, and it is impossible to say how many subscribers helped.

Some 80 per cent of the grants went to Church of England schools, and it is certain that this was an unfair proportion. The Church had the advantage of a countrywide organisation and was in a position to found more schools. It is also probable that it had the more wealthy and willing subscribers. Expenditure is not a sure way of measuring effective results, because money can be wasted; but we do know that the improvements in the training colleges and other methods of promoting the qualifications of teachers sprang largely from the work of the Committee of Privy Council, inspired by the ideals of Kay-Shuttleworth. By 1870 grants towards the building of these colleges had reached a total of £115,000. Between 1850 and 1860 the number of certificated teachers increased from 1,093 to 6,433, and by 1870 the number was 12,744. There had been a lesser increase in the number of pupil teachers because the first effects of the Revised Code was to reduce the attractions of the profession. The number of inspected schools increased by four and a half times in these twenty years, with the net result of more qualified teachers per school. As the average attendance only increased four and a half times and the number of pupil teachers three and a half times, this meant quite a considerable improvement in the staffing ratio.

The educational expansion did not show improved results in all directions. It was generally accepted that the schools tended to draw pupils of a higher social standard than they were meant to do, and in the reports sent to the Newcastle Commission there was serious criticism of the teachers for paying too much attention to the brighter scholars. Some of the Inspectors who made these observations later regretted what they had said, for they thought that the Commissioners had paid too much attention to this criticism.

The figures for average attendance could conceal many factors. There could be more children on the roll and a decline in the number of attendances made by each one. There could also be a change in the age groups of the children and it was found that the proportion of children under ten years of age had increased by 10 per cent in the period 1850–7, and for children under eight years the increase was even more marked. The capitation grants beginning in 1853 were a part cause of this influx of younger children, but it is also true that the demand for child labour was rising as factory methods spread to other occupations, so that the proportion of older children was less. While the Factory Acts, because of their troublesome conditions, had their influence in limiting the number at work in the controlled factories, children above the age of nine were not seriously affected because they could find other work in uncontrolled employments. The figures also show that under the age of ten there were more boys at school than girls, because the girls were more useful at home, but in the ten to fifteen age group the position was reversed, the girls at school being in a majority.

When measured by the capitation grants the average attendance was only 41 per cent. According to present-day standards this is very low, but the habit of sending a child regularly to school takes time to establish and, as previously mentioned, if a child was away on Monday he tended to stay away the whole week so that the weekly school fee could be saved. The grants were based on an attendance of 192 days in the year; this amounts to four days a week for forty-eight weeks, though sixteen days were allowed for absences. The half-time children earned the grant for attendances on eighty-eight days and the evening scholars for fifty nights, and as they were included in the 41 per cent average this would affect the figures. When the Revised Code was introduced the grants for half-timers were given, after examination, to those who had made one hundred attendances, or twenty-four for evening classes.

These statistics are not conclusive, because children changed from one school to another, sometimes because parents moved away, but sometimes because of the whims of parents or children. The surplus in school accommodation was 40 per cent more than the average attendance in 1851 and about 60 per cent in 1870. Sometimes this was an incentive to teachers to poach children from other schools, and occasionally they lowered school fees in competition to achieve their purpose. If the figures are reliable, only 59 per cent of children stayed more than one year at the same school and 20 per cent for three years and over. These percentages must be qualified, as some children would pass from one school to another or from grant-aided schools to private schools, so that accuracy is not possible. There is no doubt that irregular attendance and the change from one school to another seriously reduced the real value of the money spent on education. Despite the hopes of some theorists, better teachers and better schools did not have the desired effects of increasing educational demand.

The numerical facts must be used with great caution, although the politicians of the period used them as the basis of 'conclusive arguments'. The figures given in the Report of the Newcastle Commission are generally given to the unit and the decimals to two places, yet most of these figures were arrived at by an exhaustive analysis of ten specimen districts and then multiplied by a factor to make them apply nationally. Besides this, all the Assistant Commissioners who collected statistics expressed their doubts about the correctness of their own figures and the tendency of enthusiasts to inflate figures to prove an argument must be allowed for.

The Committee of Privy Council

The growth of the system is a partial expression of public opinion, particularly as public expenditure affects all taxpayers; but contemporary criticism must be considered as well. For politicians it centred first on the character of the Committee of Privy Council. As a Committee it rarely functioned effectively, as it tended to endorse all proposals put before it. The principal members were the Lord President and, from 1856, the Vice-President. Sometimes the latter caught all the limelight, particularly as he was in the Commons, but on occasion the former asserted his responsibility. As with many other departments of the period it did not owe its powers to statute, but unlike other departments, which operated in strictly defined fields or through Local Boards such as the Poor Law, the Education Department was making the first governmental experiment in national social administration. There was only one real Parliamentary occasion when the policy of the Department could be criticised and that was when the annual estimates were submitted to the House. Yet educational growth seemed so insignificant that no Minister was put on trial for his educational policy—the resignation of Robert Lowe in 1864 being a result of his pride and the jubilant attacks of his enemies, not a matter of major policy.

The Committee of Privy Council did not, however, escape the criticism of being despotic. When it altered the conditions attached to the grants there were repercussions all over the country and M.P.s were not slow to press the demands of their voters for reconsideration. In general, apart from the Management Clauses, the Conscience Clause and the Revised Code, there was little ground for complaint as the schools were on the whole gaining financially. True, the Committee had a stormy start in 1839 and the House of Lords protested 'that the powers thus intrusted to the Committee of Council are so important in their bearing upon the moral and religious education of the people of this country and upon the proper duties and functions of the Established Church, and at the same time are capable of progressive and indefinite extension, that they ought not to be committed to any public authority without the consent of Parliament'.[1] This consent was to some extent given when an Act was passed in 1856 creating the position of Vice-President; nevertheless the fear of progressive and indefinite extension noted by the House of Lords was not unjustified. Peel, who had more foresight than many, said in a letter of 1842 to Sir James Graham, a member of his Government, that a more rapid advance in promoting good education would be made 'by a cautious and gradual extension of the power and pecuniary means of the Committee of Privy Council than by any announcement at present of any plan by the Government'.[2] Sir John Pakington, who was one of the most active of Conservatives in pressing for better educational provisions, said on the first reading of his Bill of 1855: 'While I am anxious to place increased powers in the hands of the educational department of the State, I must beg at the same time to state that I am not content to place these powers in the hands of the Committee of Council as it is at present constituted.' In pressing for the appointment of a Royal Commission in 1858 and in a draft report for a Select Committee in 1866 he made similar criticisms.[3]

One result of the Royal Commission was the Revised Code, which led to the printing of numerous pamphlets and articles emphasising the despotic character of the Committee; but its powers continued unchecked despite the large and important representative deputation in 1862 to Lord Palmerston the Prime Minister, to press home its charges. Even the *Annual Register* of 1862, which gave more space to the weather in that year than to education, entered into the fray. Some critics went so far as to argue in favour of free trade in education and the abolition of all state powers. 'In commerce they were told free trade was a sound principle. Why then could not the hon. Gentleman trust competition in this matter of education?' said Mr B. Hope, a Conservative, in a debate on 22 May 1851, taunting Hume the free trader. Robert Lowe in 1858 was more explicit: 'The people unfortunately had a very strong taste for fermented liquors. The demand created the supply, and at every corner there was a gin palace to minister to their wants. If there were the same taste for education there would be no need for any Government machinery to supply it. It might be Utopian to suppose that there ever would be such a taste, but was it not right to do all they could to stimulate the desire for education, that when once created they might dispense with the necessity of any Government aid.'[4]

The policy of the Committee of Privy Council was more strongly attacked on the ground that poor districts were neglected. The education building grants were based on the principle of self-help, and in poverty-stricken areas, or where the people of means were not interested, no schools were built. Where most of the local population were indigent Irish immigrants the Roman Catholics had an up-hill task in finding money to build schools. They could not even qualify for a Government building grant unless most of the money was raised locally. 'The Government grant gave least help where most was wanted', said W. J. Fox in the debate of 22 May 1851; or as *The Times* said more poetically five years later: 'We give light to the enlightened and leave the blind in total darkness.'

This led to the criticism that the state was giving help to those of a higher class who had no right to assistance. In 1862 Baines 'believed that, to a very large extent, the enormous grant of £800,000 was at present lavished upon schools where the parents were perfectly able to pay for the education of their children'.[5] Many rural schools claimed that they were too poor to qualify for grants, though for three years from 1853 they had the advantage of a special capitation grant, which was then extended to all schools. They were allowed a concession under the Revised Code of organising two to six rural schools under one head teacher instead of one certificated teacher for each school, which was a requirement elsewhere; but the concession was not widely adopted. The schools in the poor areas were particularly liable to wide variations in the school income due to economic causes, and the Newcastle Commission reported that it was 'easier to get a school built than to get it supported, and there is more evidence that the Government grants promote subscriptions for the former than for the latter purpose'. The introduction of the Revised Code altered the position completely, for the annual grant depended on an uncertain examination result. This led to an increase of school fees and sometimes the managers, contrary to the regulations, farmed the school out to the teacher to make as much profit as he could. The Education Department, on the other hand, fondly expected the managers to reduce the teachers' pay if the examination results did not come up to scratch and in this way the Newcastle Commission hoped 'to find some constant and stringent motive to induce them to do that part of their duty which is at once most unpleasant and most important'.

Teachers and over-education

Men of all political parties in the House of Commons in the 1840s thought that special steps should be taken to improve the position of teachers and to attract better men to the work for 'the supply of masters properly qualified is at the root of the whole system'. (Peel, 1845). The Minutes of 1846 went a long way to meet this need, in contrast to the Planning Act of 1947, which gave vast powers to untrained officials. The system in general met with whole-hearted approval, but as early as 1850 it was said that many young teachers were entering into holy orders and that this was a proof of their qualifications being too high. The Earl of Harrowby in a debate on July 1850 said 'he did not want to establish schoolmasters as servants of the state, because if they (i.e. the Government) created the feeling on their part that they stood in that position, they would be in danger of losing that humility which was so desirable in them'.[6] Even Sir John Pakington, an educational enthusiast, said in 1855 that 'the masters are so overtrained that they are, in too many cases, above educational duties, and they take to other pursuits'.[7] The Newcastle Commission found a mine of information about defective teaching in the reports of the Inspectors, though the latter said their criticisms were intended to be helpful and not to damn the system.

The examination standards of the Revised Code were intended to remedy the defect of over-education, but the position of the certificated teacher was also threatened. 'It might be said of the schoolmaster, as it had been said of the poet, *Nascitur non fit*. . . . He would, therefore, throw the competition for masters perfectly open, without regard to training schools'—such was the belief of W. J. Fox expressed in a debate of 1850. Ten years later the idea was taken up by many, both in and out of Parliament. Mr Walter, proprietor of *The Times*, moved a resolution in the House in 1862 which was narrowly lost, that to require the employment of certificated teachers and pupil teachers 'is inexpedient and inconsistent with the principle of payment for results'.[8] The subject was raised again and again in the next few years, particularly because the costliness of the trained teacher made it impossible for poor schools to earn the grant. Robert Lowe, for once on the side of the teachers, defended the policy of certification on the analogy of examinations for attorneys, medical men and sea captains—'Does anybody conceive that these are violations of free trade?' he asked. Edwin Chadwick reported that 'upwards of 700 returns from unexamined and uncertificated teachers to the Census Commissioners (of 1861) are signed with marks only'. Yet a majority of the Select Committee on Education of 1865 was in favour of payment by results alone, although this was not supported by the official witnesses.

The Committee of Privy Council did not drop its requirement that teachers in grant-earning schools should be certificated, and when the Revised Code led to a reduction in their number and a fall of 5,000 (= 35 per cent) in the number of pupil teachers, it approved a Minute in 1867 which reversed the trend; from then on the numbers of trained teachers and pupil teache.. began once more to increase.

The complaint of over-education was also extended to the pupil teachers. In a debate of June 1854 Lord Seymour said that: 'it seemed to him we were raising up a very large class of pupil teachers, and he did not see how hereafter they were to find employment. You gave them an education above their class, and they were then of course unwilling to go back to labour, looking for some better position. . . . You were raising up what would be a discontented class of persons throughout the country.'[9] Lord John Russell earlier in the debate expressed the opposite view. 'But the benefit derived from these pupil teachers had not been confined solely to [the schools]. The poorer classes have derived great benefit from their sons receiving incomes averaging about £18 per annum for their merit and talent and the parents have considered themselves raised in the social scale from these advantages.'[10]

The over-education of scholars was also criticised. The education of pauper children was said to be better than that of rate paying labourers. Others in reply said that in any case children left school too soon for them to be over-educated or unfitted for their future course in life, but the Newcastle Commission was convinced that over-education was the real problem.

The need for improvement

Until the census of 1851 it was generally thought that the employment of children was the main cause of poor attendance at schools. However, the published figures showed that there were large numbers of children neither at school nor at work, while the schools themselves were only half full. The parents were therefore to blame because of this indifference unless they were too poor to pay the school fees. Some hoped that adult education would show the parents the value of school for their children, but it was generally admitted that such adult classes intended for the working classes were soon usurped by the middle classes. In some areas they experimented with money prizes for good attendance and even the Committee of Privy Council in 1855 proposed to issue attendance certificates to scholars over twelve who had stayed three years at the same school and reached a certain standard. In some schools children who earned the capitation grant had part of it paid to them, while the others whose attendance was bad were required to pay higher school fees. These educational condiments were praised for a time, but in the end they failed.

In the 1850s the Inspectors reported that there was a decline in the average age of the children in school and one of them was so pessimistic about this that he compared 'the long and imposing array of certificated masters and mistresses . . . all the instructive books—all the excellent maps, all the ingenious apparatus to a park of artillery for the dispersion of a flock of sparrows'.[11] The real cause of the fall in average age was the considerable increase in the number of younger children in the schools, partly caused by the capitation grants. For a time the Inspectors thought the decline was due to the excellence of the teaching so that children had learnt all that was necessary at a younger age, but later they came to realise that this argument was not valid.

Evening schools were considered as a possible remedy for the early leaving age and the first Minute giving grants was approved in 1855. In 1862 this reached a maximum of £2,192 paid in the form of annual grants to teachers of £5 or £10; this shows that there were less than 450 classes. The Revised Code altered the system of grants and by 1870 £26,100 was reached and an average attendance of 73,000. Grants were paid for scholars over twelve but it was possible to present a pupil a second time in the same or even a lower standard, so that the results showed no advance over the day schools.

The provision of infant schools was another remedy put forward, and the Newcastle Commission even proposed schools for those aged three to seven years. The Revised Code paid grants without examination for those under six and therefore the schools gained financially; this led to an increase of about 3 per cent in the proportion of children under six from 1860 to 1870.

Neither night schools nor infant schools solved the problems of irregular attendance. The Manchester Education Aid Society, founded in 1864, gave financial help where it was considered parents could not afford to pay school fees but half the parents who were entitled to aid were too indifferent to apply for it. Since half the children of the three to twelve age group were neither at school nor at work and as the Society had eliminated poverty as a cause, then parental neglect was shown to be the main cause of non attendance. Thus the only possible remedy was a law for compulsory attendance.

The Times in 1859 described the state of contemporary opinion with considerable insight. 'To us the question of education seems to be in the position so admirably expressed by the denunciation "Woe unto ye when all men speak well of you". All men speak well of education, some certainly from real conviction, others because they think quite enough has been done, and wish to persuade us to be content with what we have . . . and others because, having laboured long in the cause, they cannot bear to admit to themselves that it has not attained the amount of success to which they think it entitled.'[12]

One result of the growing expenditure of the Privy Council was to promote the jealousy of the middle classes, just as honest labourers had been jealous of the education of pauper children. The Earl of Harrowby in 1850 said in Parliament that 'they were attempting to give the children in these schools too ambitious an education and the result was showing itself in the objections of the middle classes . . . [who] complained that their children were being displaced by those who were getting, at the expense of the State, a better education than they could procure for their own children'.[13] The Inspectors frequently referred to this in their reports following 1850 and one Inspector said that since the middle classes largely controlled the machinery of local government this hindered the use of local agencies for educational development. This was shown particularly in the parsimonious attitude of the Guardians to the education of pauper children.

Between 1860 and 1867 the discussion on the problem of education for the middle classes almost eclipsed that of the education of poor children, except for arguments over the Revised Code and the Conscience Clause. The Public Schools Commission (1961–4) and the Schools Enquiry Commission (1964–7) attracted a good deal of attention and the newspapers as well as the National Society for the Promotion of Social Science dwelt much on this subject. As yet there was no practical suggestion that the state should give aid to secondary schools, but the elementary schools did not lose by this wider interest in the matter.

Although a small minority on the Newcastle Commission hoped that state aid might slowly disappear, it seems clear that state assistance for the education of the poor was firmly established by 1850. The growth of the system stimulated criticism and criticism stimulated the growth of the system. Rarely did the critics express a hope that the system would be utterly destroyed and they were content to point out its failures; in the enumeration of these defects they implicitly accepted the principle of state aid. Education was not only good in itself but it had utilitarian advantages for the state and these utilitarian arguments, together with those of the Radical politicians, will be considered in the next chapter.

REFERENCES

1. Hans. 30 June 1854, vol. 134, c. 967–8, quotation by Miall.
2. C. S. Parker, *Sir James Graham*, vol. 1, p. 340.
3. Hans. 16 Mar. 1855, vol. 137, c. 646, and 11 Feb. 1858, vol. 148, c. 1195–6; and PP 1866, vol. 7, p. 117 and pp. ix–xi.
4. Hans. 21 June 1858, vol. 151, c. 150.
5. Hans. 27 Mar. 1862, vol. 166, c. 195.
6. Hans. 2 July 1850, vol. 112, c. 823; Lord Harrowby also feared that teachers would become preachers of discontent, and pointed to the revolutions in Europe, 1848–50.
7. Hans. 16 Mar. 1855, vol. 137, c. 645.
8. Hans. 5 May 1862, vol. 166, c. 1257. He moved a similar resolution 5 May 1863.
9. Hans. 30 June 1854, vol. 134, c. 977.
10. Hans. 30 June 1854, vol. 134, c. 960.
11. PP 1854–5, vol. 42, p. 439.
12. *The Times*, 12 Nov. 1859.
13. Hans. 2 July 1850, vol. 112, c. 821.

6

The Political Arguments

The expediency of education

It is unlikely that a national referendum, in 1870 would have yielded an answer favourable to the establishment of a system of state education, yet there were ideas and arguments circulating among members of Parliament which in the end convinced them that the Act of 1870, incomplete as it was, could be justified. The religious arguments played their part; the arguments based on the need to do something with the haphazard system which had grown up were important; but the arguments based on the expediency of some form of state education probably carried most conviction.

The Radical thinkers tried to prove that something more was required than the expansion of denominational efforts, aided by government grants, and argued that if the nation was to be responsible it could not leave the control of expenditure in the hands of voluntary societies. The growing control of the state over the universities at the present time is an example of a well-worn path in the expansion of our scholastic system. The utilitarian arguments probably carried most weight, but the theories of politicians, aided in some cases by a political philosophy, had some value.

Thomas Carlyle wrote in his book on Chartism in 1839: 'Education is not only an eternal duty, but has at length become even a temporary and ephemeral one, which the necessities of the hour will oblige us to look after.'[1] Sir James Graham, Home Secretary in Peel's government, said to the Prime Minister in 1842 about a letter from Kay-Shuttleworth: 'Every man has his nostrum. The Clerk of the Council for Education thinks that moral training and normal schools will restore peace. These instruments are not to be despised, and have too long been neglected; but cheap bread ... will have a more pacifying effect than all the mental culture which any Government can supply.'[2] 'We live in an age', wrote the Vicar of Leeds in 1846, 'when the question is not *whether* but *how* the poor are to be edu-

74

cated.' At the meeting of the Social Science Association in 1858 Lord Brougham said 'the days had long gone by when it was deemed necessary for the peace of society first, that learning in general, then at any rate political science, should be confined to the upper orders of the community, as if the humble ranks were either incapable of comprehending it or to be entrusted with it.'[3]

There were many reasons for this general acceptance of the policy of educating the poor, but at the basis of most of them was the idea of political expediency. Crime and pauperism seemed to be on the increase, strikes and riots to be more common, England's manufacturing supremacy seemed to be challenged by other nations whose technical schools were said to be better, and the political stability of the country seemed to depend more and more on the education of the masses.

The idea of the perfectability of man which was beginning to find expression in the late eighteenth century, was the keystone of Radical opinion in the nineteenth century. Education would cure the evil spirit in man and this would pave the way for the new society when crime and pauperism would be no more. Until the Poor Law of 1834 the ruling classes of the previous generation had been obsessed by the growth in pauperism and the constant fear of an increase in the poor rates; this fear was strong even in the 1890s. No doubt the return of soldiers from the Napoleonic wars was a part cause of the increase in crime, but the strikes and riots in the industrial areas and the rick-burning in the country was probably due to profound social unrest, influenced by the revolutions in France and elsewhere in Europe, as well as by the social upheaval in Britain.

Many of the earlier writers on this subject were at pains to show that the great majority of criminals were uneducated. Sir John Pakington in 1855 compared the criminal statistics of Austria with those of England and showed 'that in Austria, which is one of the best educated countries of Europe, crime is greatly less than in England'. The fact that juvenile crime was still increasing despite the spread of education was met by the argument of W. J. Fox in 1850 'that education as now administered had had comparatively little effect on the abatement of crime'. 'To talk of training the character of a child by giving him twelve or fifteen months of desultory schooling before he is ten years old, is a cruel mockery. It may give him the knowledge of good and evil, but it cannot possibly train him to hate the evil and love the good. He is sent forth as he came, with his passions unsubdued; the only difference being that his wits have been sharpened for the devil's service. . . . You have taught him to write that he may one day sign

75

his name in a prison register to the scandal of education;'[4]—such were the views of an Inspector, writing in 1852. Lord Ashley thought that want of education 'was not the only nor the chief source of crime', which he attributed to want of employment. Another MP said 'The true object of education was not to make men learned but to make them good men and good subjects'.[5]

Radical Views

This sceptical view was not generally accepted. The Radical Hume argued that 'as they had put an end (in 1853) to the transportation of convicts, they must provide some means, either of taking care of them in this country or of reducing their number. Now he looked upon a proper plan of really national instruction, as the best and surest means of effecting the latter and more desirable of these objects.'[6] Many of the old Conservatives urged the need for such schools once it was realized that, apart from the Ragged Schools, government aid hardly touched that class of children which 'swarmed in our courts and alleys' and from which the 'criminal population was recruited. . . . It would be better', said Henley in 1856, 'to bring a large area of the population within the pale of educational influences than to plume ourselves upon the high standard of instruction we imparted to a limited number'.

The revival of interest in the schools after 1865 led to a repetition of the former arguments: 'Would not the policemen be better employed in assisting the work of the schoolmaster by collecting together for school attendance the wilfully neglected children, who are springing up into recruits for the great army of crime?' asked Mr Henry Cartwright at the Social Science Association of 1867. 'Compulsory attendance', said Henry Fawcett, 'once facilitating the education of children now neglected, crime and pauperism would infallibly be diminished. . . . This argument would not fail to commend itself to the rate payers.'[7] The Radicals insisted that at the same time the standard of education must be considerably improved to achieve this end, while the Denominationalists emphasised the need for a truly religious basis if moral training was to be effective. This led to the argument for compulsory education: 'Where the conditions of life of any class of children are such that their existence under these conditions is a positive nuisance to the community, the state evidently has a right to interfere to compel their parents to prevent their being thus a nuisance, and to train them up properly',[8] argued the Rev. H. Sandford in 1868.

Crime and pauperism were always associated in the nineteenth century. Pauperism, it was thought, was as much the result of moral depravity as crime. The 'worthy poor' would get help from voluntary societies, but the depraved had no claim upon society. The teaching of pauper children was one of the first educational duties recognised by the state, but the earliest Poor Law schools were severely criticised by the Inspectors; they condemned the association of children with adult paupers, particularly when one of the latter was used as the schoolmaster. Parochial Union schools were advocated so that children could be separated from adults and taught in their own schools. In the *Edinburgh Magazine* of April 1861 it is reported that the education given in the Parochial Union School at Slough was superior to that given at the neighbouring College of Eton; unfortunately religious education was neglected at the Parochial School, so that the moral depravity of the one was equal to that of the other. The Guardians, however, showed no desire to spend the rates in this way and it was hoped that by an Act of 1862 they might be encouraged to send the children to be educated at the local day schools; but this Act was largely a dead letter. Denison's Act of 1855 gave the power to pay for the education of outdoor paupers, but not as a condition of receiving outdoor relief. It was not unusual, however, for the Guardians to refuse outdoor relief if the children were kept at school and not sent to work. The powers given in this Act were very little used and the education of workhouse children developed along separate lines with a separate training school for poor law teachers with its own teachers' certificate. The aim was to emphasise the importance of practical education, more particularly of country or domestic pursuits. The purity of country life and rural activities as opposed to the more criminal life of industrial towns is a noticeable opinion in many cultures.

These ideas for the improvement of pauper education were contemporary with legislation for Reformatory and Industrial schools. These schools were universally approved, thus showing that education as a cure for crime and pauperism was generally accepted. The emphasis laid on practical instruction and the dangers of over education was in part a result of this reliance on the preventive aspect of education. The educational standards of the Revised Code were considered more than sufficient for the eradication of criminal and pauper tendencies while practical teaching ensured that no one had an excuse for being unskilled and unemployed.

Education was not only praised for its moral and social effects but also for its economic benefits. During the nineteenth century the wealthy industrialists assumed more and more importance in domestic

77

politics; they not only invaded the House of Commons but also gained a few seats in the House of Lords. In the second generation, if not in the first, a wealthy man found the doors to the peerage were not firmly closed, even when his wealth was not derived from land. It was found difficult to interest employers in education because the schools deprived them of a source of cheap labour and the half-time system was found to be very troublesome. To win their support it was argued that education would prevent strikes, particularly if political economy were taught. 'What class was the most interested in educating the people?' asked one member of the Commons in 1854; 'Why, the wealthy class; for how could capital, how could religion, how could free institutions be safe with an ignorant population?'[9] Richard Cobden used similar arguments in speeches made in this period. Walter Bagehot, writing in 1848 on Mill's *Principles of Political Economy*, said: '. . . the intelligence of the workmen employed in agriculture and still more in manufactures is an important element in the efficiency of industry.' 'Every day', said one Inspector in 1854, 'the special education of English workmen is becoming a commercial question of the deepest importance.' In the same year an agricultural expert wrote in *The Times*: 'Of the mass of machines exhibited, how few are accessible to the great body of occupying tenants, and how many, even if placed in their hands, have in their labourers the skill and the patience to work and keep them in order?'[10] This argument in favour of state intervention was turned on its head by one ingenious politician who, in 1856, said that with the introduction of machinery and the appointment to the Civil Service posts by open competition, the demand for education would increase of its own accord. 'He could not help thinking that they might look with far greater confidence to the operation of these natural causes than to any compulsory enactment for the extension of that great blessing.'[11]

By 1867 the industrial and commercial competition of other countries was being keenly felt and the demand for industrial education increased. Huxley, in an address to the South London Working Men's College in 1868, mentioned three classes of men who favoured education: 'Politicians would educate their masters, manufacturers wanted more efficient hands, the clergy desire to stem the drift towards infidelity.'[11A] Even success in war was attributed to education and the defeat of the French by the Prussians was a testimony to the superior education of the latter—an argument which was common in 1870. Education would not only help the manufacturer to increase his profits, but it would aid his wife in the management of her household. The Rev. R. Gurney, Clerical Secretary of the Church of England

Education Society, suggested to members of the Social Science Association of 1859 that in girls' schools the industrial element should be 'more largely introduced, so that we might look to them with more hope for a better and higher principled class of houshold servants than they now furnish'.

The commercial and industrial values attributed to education were not so great as their political significance. The French Revolution was contemporary with politicians of the early nineteenth century, and other European revolutions in the years up to 1851 led many to think that strikes and riots in England were a prelude to a Reign of Terror. Part of the success of the movement towards universal education was due to the belief that good schools would make the people more peaceful. Kay-Shuttleworth in 1839 said good secular education would be an antidote to the dangers of Chartism. Lord John Russell and Gladstone saw in the comparative peacefulness in England the value of the educational system. Sir Robert Inglis, a Tory diehard, did not undervalue the state of education which had preserved England from the continental troubles of the years 1848 to 1850, though he 'did not regard mere knowledge in itself as a benefit, but rather as an unmixed evil, when unsanctified by the blessing of God'.[12] The argument was thus used to prove that the foreign systems were not as good as the English system, contrary to the view of the Radicals who wanted reform and quoted foreign examples to that end.

The Radical politicians praised the more positive values and Hume maintained that 'it was due to the children of this country—it was due to the state, and it was due to themselves, to provide that the children of the working classes should not grow up to manhood ignorant of the principles, a knowledge of which would enable and induce them to support the institutions of the country in peace and in war: or, if they differed from and wished to change those institutions, to enable them to support the grounds on which they proceeded with valid and rational arguments'[13]—a view which not all members of the House of Commons would swallow in 1843. By 1856 the Liberals, and some Conservatives, were beginning to accept the Radical theory, and even Lord Robert Cecil echoed their views. As the year 1867 approached the emphasis on education and the vote became more marked—and perhaps there is an analogy in the Franchise Acts of 1918 and 1928 with the Education Acts of the period. Speaking at Rochdale in 1859, Richard Cobden pointed out how education and the franchise had gone hand in hand in America. 'One of the advantages which I expect to see derived from the wide extension of the franchise in this country is that there will be increased attention paid by those who are in influential places to the promotion of national education.'[14] We must educate our masters was the theme of Robert Lowe, the Whig, when the vote was extended in 1867 and the cry was taken up by most of the Conservatives. The Radicals did not always welcome their new allies and many of them deplored the narrow scope of the Education Bill. 'Perhaps it would not be charitable to inquire too closely into all the motives which may have led the upper and middle classes to interest themselves so suddenly and so largely in the education of the poor. Indeed if the immediate education of our masters is necessary for the safe working of the present constitution, the present generation of ignorance is quite enough to effect its ruin'[15]—so said one of the Radicals in the debates of 1870.

The arguments of the Radicals, which tended to emphasize the practical value of education for the lower orders, inclined to a materialist view of the educational purpose of the state. If it is difficult to feel patient with the supporters of religious education because they hindered the growth of a national system, it is also true that their religious ideals were more highly perfected than the social ideals of their opponents and truly religious people valued education as something more than a political, economic and social purgative. The arguments which proved that education was expedient emphasised too much its preventive value and its creative value was neglected; this is shown particularly in the Revised Code.

One of the most important political problems was the relationship between the state and the parent. In the early nineteenth century bureaucratic administration was distrusted, and therefore the development of Voluntary Schools fitted in with the accepted political philosophy. *The Times* rejoiced in the failure of Lord John Russell's educational proposals of 1856: 'What we do for ourselves we generally do well; what is done for us by our Government is as universally ill done.' Private munificence called out the compassion of the rich for the poor. 'We shall lose some of the most precious cement of society', said the H.M.I. Archdeacon Allen in 1858, 'if the relations now established through the school, between the clergymen, the landowner, the tradesman and the children of the poor be weakened'. Edward Baines, the Voluntaryist, argued in 1852 that a rate-aided system would be 'more likely to pauperise a community than the bestowment of that benevolence which is both free and specially sanctified by being religious in character, and the least humiliating and the least degrading form in which benevolence can be bestowed'.[16] Or as Gladstone put it in 1856—the voluntary system gave 'heart and love and moral influence' and therefore was to be preferred to state aid.

The Radicals, on the other hand, believed in the power of the state to achieve social reform, and in some respects they had allies among the Conservatives, such as Lord Ashley, who worked hard for social legislation, though a strong supporter of religious education. Brougham, Roebuck, Owen, Lovett and Cobden were each in their time a leader of Radical thought and all strongly believed in national education. It was not from the faiths of parsons and ministers, nor from the theories of political economists that the idea of political education took root, but from the beliefs of these Radicals, some of whom were actively employed in teaching and managing schools in the towns. But by 1852, when Chartism was already a dead force, 'a very considerable number of the earnest friends of education', wrote Horace Mann, 'gradually came to the conclusion that the increase and improvement of our popular day schools would be best promoted without any intervention by the State'.[17] The Chartist fiasco of 1848 and the failure of the contemporary revolutions in Europe did much to stifle Radical ideas, and the increasing prosperity of the country and the abandonment by the newly enfranchised middle classes of their early espousal of the cause of labour led the working classes to turn from political to economic activities. Some of the leading spirits among working men also emigrated and the leavening ideas of political reform were weakened.

The Churches and education

When the educational ideals of the Radicals again became an active force in the 1860s, they revived their plans for a secular system administered by the state. While most of the Churches placed religious teaching in the forefront of their schemes and argued that there could be no real education through secular subjects alone, the secularists thought that the work of religious teaching could be left to the Churches to carry out in their own time with the benefit gained from the reading and writing taught in the schools. To some it was a question of religious liberty, either the liberty to choose a denominational school (the basic argument of the Catholics) or the liberty to receive education without any proselytism or religious bias, the fundamental argument of the Radicals.

Parliament rejected all Bills proposing secular education and favoured the arguments of the Denominationalists, even to the point of refusing government grants to secular schools. The Act of 1870 made it possible for secular schools to receive grants for the first time, but the School Boards did not show any marked favour for this type of school. On the other hand, from the very first, the Inspectors were forbidden to inspect religious education and the Revised Code did not include it as a subject for which grants could be paid. The Conscience Clause was the safeguard which the governments applied to protect religious liberty, though this provoked much opposition among some Churchmen. It was applied in the Endowed Schools Act of 1869, and this foreshadowed its inclusion in the Act of 1870.

The policy of unsectarian religious education was supported by some Nonconformists and Churchmen, but not by Roman Catholics, as a possible compromise. The Education League formed in 1869 campaigned for unsectarian schools and had the support of many of the Radicals, but after the Act of 1870 was passed, because it seemed to them too biased in favour of denominationalism, it changed to a policy of secularism. John Stuart Mill would have preferred to defeat an Education Bill which was not secular, though he would have waived all his other objections if that could be achieved. In the end unsectarianism has prevailed and the Education Act of 1944 gave its approval to the many-agreed syllabuses of religious education which had been framed in the years after 1920. Only the Roman Catholics and a few Church schools have taken a strong line in favour of dogmatic religious teaching.

The Churches and the state were more careful of the tender religious consciences than they need have been. Many parents were indifferent or even sent their children to the school they considered best regardless of its religious teaching, and this is still true today of girls' convent schools. The duty of the state to secure education for children seemed, however, to be contradicted by the argument in favour of the liberty of the parent. Dr Hook, Archdeacon of Chichester, who had been an ardent educationist for many years, said in 1865: 'We talk of the rights of men, the rights of women; let us clamour for the rights of babes.'[18] John Ruskin said that it was 'the first duty of a state to see that every child born therein shall be well housed, clothed, fed and educated till it attain years of discretion.'[19] The Rev. Charles Kingsley and John Stuart Mill, with reservations, expressed similar views.

The duty of parents : compulsory and free education

Conservatives admitted the right of the child but placed the primary duty on the parents. If the parent failed, then it was the duty of the religious congregations, said Kay-Shuttleworth; only in the last resort, he thought, should the Christian state intervene. One speaker at the Social Science congress of 1860 complained that among ignorant parents 'the idea has of late largely grown up . . . and has even been uttered in Parliament, that if the state insists on the parent educating his child he may insist on the state feeding it'.[20]

If the state had a duty to ensure that children were educated, there seemed to be no alternative to compulsory education, and this was another challenge to the rights of parents. At one time it was thought that if only schools were free there would be scholars in abundance, but the experience of Inspectors showed that free schools were unsuccessful. Others hoped that by regulating child labour children would either be at school half-time under the Factory Acts or would be free for full-time schooling. But again experience proved that this would not work. It was even suggested that an improvement in the quality of teaching would attract more children, but this proved of no avail. Only as a last resort was the idea of compulsory education gradually accepted. Many of the Radicals had favoured this proposal from the beginning and had pointed to examples in foreign countries such as Germany and Switzerland, but the Earl of Shaftesbury in his presidential address to the Social Science Association in 1859 expressed the general view: 'In masses of population such as ours there will ever be many thousands, who, from a variety of causes will never enter any school at all. . . . Though in many districts there are schools enough, very many children are never sent to them, and, except under compulsion by law (which God forbid) never will be.'[21]

The problem of compulsion was specially considered by the Newcastle Commission and it reported that the general feeling did not favour compulsion on political, social or religious grounds, mainly because the system was advancing successfully without it. Sir James Graham's opinion was that 'pains and penalties will never educate the people of England'. In his essay *On Liberty* John Stuart Mill argued in favour of the rights of the child to education, but was opposed to the control of schools by the state. He was convinced that the laws of demand and supply could not be relied upon. Compulsory powers were not unknown to the law for they applied to pauper children in the workhouse, to factory children in some regulated industries, to children attending Industrial and Reformatory schools and to a lesser extent to the children of soldiers and sailors. In a letter to *The Times* in 1856 Charles Vansittart said that the liberty of the subject was already infringed by Vaccination Acts, Boards of Health, and the Ten Hours Bill; the interest of the many was the test and by this test compulsory education was a necessity.

The problem was brought to the fore by the National Education League and the National Education Union, both formed in 1869. No doubt they were inspired by the success of the Catholic Association formed by O'Connell in 1824 and the Anti-Corn Law League. The Union was the more conservative body and it had the support of Kay-Shuttleworth; it feared compulsion because it might 'produce among the people a reactionary feeling, which may defeat the very object which you have at heart'. The Earl of Harrowby, one of its leading supporters, opposed the education of all children from nine to twelve years because it was not 'compatible with the existence of labour at all or with the proper training of the labourers' children to assist in the maintenance of their families and their ultimate maintenance of themselves'.[22] Other Conservatives went a little further and only opposed compulsion until future investigations might prove it desirable.

The supporters of the League agreed with J. S. Mill, who 'did not see anything short of a legal obligation which will overcome the in-difference, the greed, or the really urgent pecuniary interest of parents'. Not a few Inspectors realised that only compulsion would cure the drawbacks of irregular attendance. The Social Science Association in 1867 reiterated that 'a compulsory primary education, which shall leave no child in this free and Christian land without the elements of knowledge, can alone satisfy the exigencies of the case'. Professor Fawcett was so strongly influenced by the ready acceptance of compulsory attendance abroad that he thought 'compulsory educa-tion, if established, would only be required for a single generation. Let the nation once be really educated and they could do without a compulsory system.'[23] Some went so far as to compare a taste for education with a taste for strong liquor.

To many Radicals free education was a corollary of compulsory edu-cation, but they found little general support for the idea. Denison's Act of 1855 recognised the need for free education for the children of the destitute on outdoor relief, but in practice the powers were rarely used by the niggardly Guardians. For a few years the free Ragged Schools received grants, but this was stopped in 1861. Lord Lyttelton in 1868 argued that the right to free education should only apply to those who had a right to free food and the stigma of pauperism should be applied; the great majority of the working classes could afford to educate their children. One Radical, who could not foresee the results of free education approved by the Act of 1891, said free education in municipal schools would not destroy the denominational schools because a stigma would attach to the free schools. But the Education

League went further and argued that to give free education only to those who put in a plea of poverty 'is really to pauperise and degrade the very class who most require to be elevated and to create invidious and baleful distinctions which will be destructive of anything like a dignified national character'.[24] One parson asked if 'people do not feel degraded by getting an eleemosynary education from the dead hand, why therefore, should they feel degraded by getting the same from the living?' 'It was a mistake', said another parson, 'to suppose that poor people felt they were being pauperised by sending their children to school, on the contrary, most of them thought they were doing the school managers a favour by patronising their institution.'[25]

Rate aid

No one thought that the state had a duty to run an educational system from its own funds and all proposals for national education included some scheme for local rates. Before 1870 all education grants had come from the government and only a few poor law schools were assisted by the rates. To create a national system mainly out of the rates was to emphasise the parallel between education and poor relief. One argument put to the Newcastle Commission in favour of rate aid was that 'education undoubtedly diminishes pauperism [and] has a direct tendency to lighten the poor rate'. There was also a very strong feeling against any kind of centralised system because it would give the government too much power, and we have since had Nazi Germany, Fascist Italy and Communist Russia as warning examples.

Local rates and local management were also favoured by the Radicals as an opportunity for local democracy. The ratepayers would be concerned with the efficiency of the schools as well as due economy of expenditure. While school fees were being paid they would also be able to balance the disadvantage of raising the rate weighed against the advantage of raising school fees. For the Government, as for all governments, local control removed many problems from the shoulders of Ministers and freed them from parliamentary questions. The dominant local religious group could also have a stronger say in school management under a local board. Some of the earlier schemes had proposed to give powers to the towns, where the education problem was more serious, but if a national scheme was to be approved, then in the absence of county councils, which were not created till 1888, local committees or boards seemed the only solution. The *ad hoc*

Board had by this time found a place in English local government, and it is not surprising that this was the solution ultimately adopted. The main objection to a rate aided system was the likelihood that it would undermine the voluntary system, which was the basis of denominational education. The local rate, said one Inspector in 1856, 'would materially weaken the missionary character which at this time pervades so much of the teaching in our schools'. The Radicals were unmoved by this argument because they hoped for more unsectarian or secular schools; 'It was said that the introduction of rating in any shape would destroy voluntary zeal; but surely this meant no more than a rating system would prove so much superior to the voluntary system that the latter would be abandoned.'[26] Milner Gibson said in 1851 that he 'had never entertained a doubt that if schools were to be supported by rates, they must not be denominational schools, must not be sectarian schools. They must be schools in which all classes of rate payers could have equal advantages.' The Bishop of Salisbury in 1853 spoke with some insight when he said he 'could not approve of such a course [a voluntary local rate] because he believed, in the first place, that it would be found nearly if not altogether inoperative; because, secondly, so far as it operated at all, it would do so only in laying the foundation of a new subject of strife and local agitation ...; and, thirdly, because he saw as its necessary consequence, a perilous interference with religious liberty, and, in the not remote future, a growing danger to religious truth'.[27] Lord Shaftesbury called the proposal 'a water rate to extinguish religious fire among young people'. Some compared an education rate with Church rates and thought it unwise and impolitic at the present time [1868], 'when they were about to abolish rating for the Church'.

The rating proposals of the Newcastle Commission were not accepted by the government partly because the method proposed gave the rating authority too little control over the money spent, but opinion in favour of rate aid was growing stronger and it found many supporters in the Social Science Association at its meeting in 1866; and by 1869 even *The Times* gave the notion mild approval. Professor Fawcett thought that 'by combining compulsory rates with compulsory attendance they would be able to convince the people that the rate was only a temporary infliction, which would be removed by the diminution of the general rates, and by increased prosperity resulting from education';[28] it will be remembered that he did not believe in free education, so that school fees would meet much of the total cost.

The demand for a national system of education came first from the Radicals. They realised that education was something more than teaching the faith of our fathers, that the citizen of the nineteenth century was unfitted for social life without education and that for each man to realise his capacities to some extent, he must be given the opportunities to develop them. They were hindered in the attempt to realise their ideals because the state and local authorities had not the organisation to cope with the administrative problems involved. Moreover, they had not the ascendancy in Parliament to combat those whose faith was based on an expansion of the existing voluntary system. The Education Act of 1870 seemed to them a defeat, but it proved to be a basis for the development of a public opinion which in the end demanded even higher educational ideals than the Radicals could have envisaged.

REFERENCES

1. Thomas Carlyle, *Chartism*, ch. 10, p. 177. 1839.
2. C. S. Parker, *Sir Robert Peel*, vol. 2, p. 541.
3. TNAPSS 1858, p. 25.
4. PP 1852–3, vol. 79, p. 353.
5. Hans. 17 July 1846, vol. 87, c. 1254. Mr. Borthwick.
6. Hans. 4 Apr. 1853, vol. 125, c. 550.
7. Hans. 12 Mar. 1869. vol. 194. c. 1221.
8. TNAPSS 1868, p. 395–6.
9. Hans. 30 June 1854, vol. 134, c. 979.
10. PP 1854, vol. 52, pp. 313–14, quoting *The Times*.
11a. Adamson, p. 317.
11. Hans. 10 Apr. 1856, vol. 141, c. 811–12.
12. Hans. 22 May 1851, vol. 116, c. 1290.
13. Hans. 25 July 1843, vol. 70, c. 1334.
14. *Speeches by Richard Cobden*, vol. 2, p. 552.
15. Hans. 15 March 1870, vol. 199, c. 1965, Winterbotham.
16. PP 1852, vol. 11, pp. 255–6: Select Committee on Manchester and Salford Education Bill.
17. PP 1852–53, vol 90, p. lxxx.
18. TNAPSS 1865, p. 56.
19. J. A. Hobson, *John Ruskin, Social Reformer*, p. 156 (1867).
20. TNAPSS 1860, p. 381, George Anderson.
21. TNAPSS 1859, pp. 14–15.
22. *The Times*, 14 Nov. 1869, report of a meeting at Manchester Town Hall.
23. Hans. 12 Mar. 1869, vol. 194, c. 1222.

7

24. A. W. Humphreys, *Robert Applegarth*, p. 202, quoting from a pamphlet.
25. TNAPSS 1869, p. 373, the Rev. Brooke Lambert.
26. Hans. 27 Apr. 1868, vol. 191, c. 1312, Earl of Kimberley.
27. Hans. 17 June 1853, vol. 128, c. 333.
28. Hans. 24 June 1868, vol. 192, c. 1998.

7

The Education Act of 1870

"An Act to provide for Public Elementary Education in England and Wales"
(The words inset are quoted from the act itself).

The provision of schools

The Education Act was different from other legislation of the reformers in the nineteenth century. It did not merely provide for inspection to see that the law was obeyed, this had been done before with the Factory Act of 1833; it did not define rights which could only be exercised occasionally as with the franchise; it was a positive law which secured school accommodation for all children whose parents did not pay a school fee exceeding nine pence a week. It was to become possible for every such child to attend an elementary school, though the government hoped that the sense of social superiority would exclude all who were not of the lower classes. Thus the Act placed the state in a new relation to society, it was not only a policeman to see that the law was carried out, it was also a teacher exercising a daily influence on the new generation of citizens. Yet, although the Act was the seed from which the system of state education has grown, many who voted for it disapproved of the organisation and administration of education by the state; they hoped that the Voluntary Schools would prove their superiority and only a few state schools would be established.

Section 5. There shall be provided for every school district a sufficient amount of accommodation in public elementary schools available for all children resident in such district.

The 1870 Act was the result of a social evil and an administrative problem; the evil was ignorance and the problem was the provision and maintenance of schools. The system which had developed since 1833 under the sponsorship of the state failed to achieve its aims and the defects of the existing scheme largely influenced the form of the Education Act. Although the Radicals hoped for an Act which would sweep away the Voluntary Schools, they were dismayed to find that, apart from London, it gave every encouragement to the denominations to build as many schools as possible before the School Boards could start building. When the Bill was introduced in the February, W. E. Forster said: 'In solving this problem there must be, consistently with the attainment of our object, the least possible expenditure of public money, the utmost endeavour not to injure existing and efficient schools, and the most careful absence of all encouragement to parents to neglect their children.'[1] In the following July he went even further: 'The opinion of the government was that it would be a very dangerous thing for them to begin, at any rate, by establishing the principle that they took upon themselves, as the state, the burden of the education of the children of any portion of the population. If they were broadly to lay down the principle that the state ought to pay the cost of the education, they would, in effect, say to the great body of parents throughout the country—"we think it our business rather than yours to educate your children", and he did not think they would be serving the cause of education by allowing such a belief to spread abroad. If the state undertook such a task the cost would be enormous. Nor would it be confined to primary education; secondary education must also be provided free.'[2]

In the original Bill the Voluntary Societies were given a year of grace to supply the deficiency in school places before the School Boards were set up. There would only be School Boards where the Education Department was satisfied, after a public enquiry, that there was insufficient accommodation. In the main the Nonconformists sided with the Radicals to protest against this concession in favour of the Church schools; in the end the year of grace was reduced to six months, and School Boards could be elected even where there was no need for new schools, but in the Metropolis, the first School Board election was to take place in 1870. In this period of grace there were 3,000 applications for building grants, compared with the previous annual average of 150. The act thus helped the Voluntary Societies to make a start with the work and limited the sphere of the School Boards. Gladstone himself said: 'I am one of those who hold that in the production of material objects it is desirable never to multiply the Establishments of the Government beyond what is necessary, but, where it is possible, to avail ourselves of private energy and zeal.'[3]

Section 3. The term 'elementary school' means a school or department of a school at which elementary education is the principal part of the education there given, and does not include any school or department of a school at which the ordinary payments in respect of the instruction, from each scholar, exceed ninepence a week.

W. E. Forster, in the debates on the Bill, pointed out that parents paid £420,000 a year in school fees (by 1891 it amounted to £1,800,000); why, he asked, 'should we relieve the parent from all payments for the education of his child? We come in and help the parents in all possible ways; but generally speaking, the enormous majority of them are able, and will continue to be able, to pay these fees.' It was no part of the policy of the Education Department to create 'comprehensive schools' and by fixing a maximum limit of ninepence a week it was hoped to restrict them to children of the manual labour class. Whether children of a better social class would have a good effect on the manners of the poorer scholars, as some Inspectors hoped, and strengthen social solidarity, or whether the bad manners of the majority would drive out the good was not discussed. One M.P., Col. Beresford, was 'entirely opposed to throwing open the schools to all classes because there are plenty of persons able to pay for the education of their children who will selfishly avail themselves of the compulsory schools and consequently the poorer rate payers will be taxed for the education of those better off'.[4] Forster argued that the schools would be left open to all children and that this was equitable where all were compelled to pay the education rates. In due course the poorer type of private school lost children to the elementary schools and children of a higher class than the small professional man and the shopkeeper (the limits which he expected would apply) turned to the public elementary schools. Col. Beresford tried to limit the elementary schools to the children of parents whose net income was below £150 per annum, but Forster opposed this because of the advantage of having all classes attending one school.

Free education and school attendance

Section 17. Every child attending a school provided by any school board shall pay such weekly fee as may be prescribed by the school board with the consent of the education department.

Section 25. The school board may, if they think fit, from time to time, for a renewable period not exceeding six months, pay the whole or any part of the school fees payable at any public elementary school. (See also Section 74 (3) for power to make bye laws on this subject.)

Section 26. If the school board satisfy the education department . . . the board may, subject to such rules and conditions as the education department may prescribe, provide such [free] school, and may admit scholars to such school without requiring any fee.

Until the Act of 1891 there was no general provision for free education in Board Schools; but exceptions were made where the parent was too poor and where a whole district was poverty stricken. The Voluntary Schools could benefit from Section 25 where the School Board thought fit, although they could not receive rate aid in any other form. This led to such an agitation against 'putting religion on the rates' that the Liberal Party lost many of its more radical supporters and this is counted as one of the main reasons for their defeat in 1874. The remedy then adopted was to transfer to the Boards of Guardians by an Act of 1876 this power to aid particular poor parents. The fact that this money also came from the rates did not seem to matter to tender consciences. *The Times* in 1870 said: 'There appears, we are glad to see, a growing disinclination to render education gratuitous', and this seemed to be the general opinion at that time. Neither the free educational ladder for the clever, nor the broad highway of free education appealed to the average politician of the period, though a few had higher aspirations. Even the Regulations of the Science and Art Department said: 'Committees of schools and classes and teachers are strongly urged (should it at present not be the practice) at once to impose as high a scale of fees as they consider can be raised not only on middle class students but also on artisans.'[5] The free bread and circuses of ancient Rome were far removed from the vision of these latter-day Victorians.

For most people free education was regarded as outside practical politics. Sir J. Pakington, ardent educationist as he was, said: 'As a question of morality, it is unquestionably desirable that the parents should be the first to make a contribution towards the education of their children.' Professor Fawcett, so radical in many of his views, considered that free education 'would dangerously weaken parental authority.' It was indeed a concession for Section 25 to provide for free education with the express proviso that it should not be deemed parochial relief. 'Parents', said Sir H. Selwin-Ibbetson, 'slighted education that was perfectly free, but learned to value and take an interest in the instruction of their children when some small payment was demanded from them.' Some expected that parents would be more interested to ensure regular attendance if they had to pay a school fee.

Section 74. Every school board may make bye laws (1) Requiring the parents of children of such age, not less than five years nor more

THE EDUCATION ACT OF 1870

than thirteen years, as may be fixed by the bye-laws, to cause such
children (unless there is some reasonable excuse) to attend school:

Any of the following reasons shall be a reasonable excuse, namely,

1. That the child is under efficient instruction in some other
   manner:
2. That the child has been prevented from attending school by
   sickness or any unavoidable cause:
3. That there is no public elementary school . . . within . . . three
   miles.

Provided that any bye-law under this section shall provide for the
total or partial exemption of such child [between 10 and 13 years of
age] from the obligation to attend school if one of Her Majesty's
Inspectors certifies that such child has reached a standard of
education specified in such bye-law.

Before 1870 laws for compulsory attendance at school only applied
to a few children, mostly those to whom the educational clauses of the
Factory Acts applied, some children of soldiers and marines, the
children in Poor Law schools and those under some legal obligation to
attend Industrial or Reformatory schools. The Radicals had great
hopes that at last they would succeed in one of their most cherished
ideas of universal compulsion, but a Liberal government put forward
conservative proposals which a Tory government might not have
risked.

It was evident from the course of the debates that Forster himself
looked forward to something more satisfactory than the permissive
powers of compulsion which the Act gave to the Schools Boards. He
supported this part of the Bill on the grounds that it was an experiment,
and that after it had been tried it would be easier to frame a law for
universal compulsion. Gladstone would not go this far and frankly
owned that it was not without an effort that he agreed to the meagre
powers to compel attendance: 'I think it is a scandal and a shame to
the country that in the midst of our, as we think, advanced civilisation,
and undoubtedly of our enormous wealth, we should at this time of
day be obliged to entertain this principle of compulsion.'[6] In 1870,
states Porter in *The Progress of the Nation*, only two-fifths of the children
between six and ten and one-fifth of those between ten and twelve
were on school registers. The Tories in the House were unanimously
opposed even to the permissive powers in the Bill. They hoped that in
the period of grace Voluntary Schools would almost satisfy the need,
so that with no School Boards there could be no bye-laws. The Bill
was, however, amended and in most of the larger boroughs School

Boards were formed, with the assent of the Education Department, and proceeded to make bye-laws even if there were no schools built by the Board.

Those who favoured indirect compulsion through laws controlling the employment of children found that they had the support of the Courts, as it was declared that bye-laws for compulsory attendance could not override the provisions of the Factory Acts. It was the ageing and philanthropic Earl of Shaftesbury who was responsible for amending the Bill to allow total or partial exemption from school for children between ages ten and thirteen years, who had reached a standard specified in the bye-laws; he preferred compulsion from age four to ten instead of five to thirteen years. Thus, after the age of ten education was subordinated to the demands of employers and the need of parents for their children's wages. However, one M.P. pointed out that 'the Inspectors reported that not more than 80,000 children throughout England obtained instruction under these [Factory] Acts; and of those 80,000 a very large proportion of them received, or were receiving, an education of so bare and transitory a character that when they reached sixteen or eighteen years of age, they forgot nearly all they had learned'. Where there were no compulsory bye-laws, and in 1877 this was true of half the population, the Factory Acts and the Agricultural Children Act of 1873 were supreme, but after the Act of 1876 children under ten (eight for farming work in some areas) could not be employed.

Sir Charles Adderley believed 'that there were many parents who would rather go to prison than take the trouble to see that their children went to school'. Even the Radical Morley 'looked with dismay to their at once setting the police to drive children into school; a great deal might be done by depriving employers of the right to employ little children'. Some thought it would be unjust to punish poor parents who sent their children to work to keep the family off the poor rates and others said compulsory education 'would fill the gaols rather than the schools'. Conversely a few agreed with Dilke that adult wages would only rise if all children were compelled to attend school. Sir Rainald Knightley argued that the parent had a right to the earnings of his children, that the mother needed someone to sit at home and mind the baby, that the infliction of fines for non-attendance would send the father to prison and the mother to the workhouse; in short, compulsory education would give rise to the impression that there was one law for the rich and another for the poor.[7]

If parental rights were of supreme importance then 'the proper object to aim at was the creation of a natural demand for education, and this would come as soon as employers sought for skilled labourers. Their object' said Adderley, 'ought to be rather to encourage and stimulate the demand than to overlay it by artificial supply. He thought compulsion was the worst way of promoting education.'[8] Some Radicals accepted this argument in part and maintained that if compulsion were applied to one generation of parents, the taste for education would be acquired and then the law could be abolished. We know today that the habit of sending children to school is very important and for many parents a compulsory law is not necessary, but a social upheaval such as that caused by the bombing of London showed that in many parents the habit was only skin deep.

> *Section 36.* Every school board may, if they think fit, appoint an officer or officers to enforce any bye-laws under this Act with reference to the attendance of children at school....

This is the origin of the School Board Man or School Attendance Officer, known today by various flowery names. Enforcement of attendance bye-laws could have been left to the police in cooperation with the headmaster, but more than one politician in the House of Commons opposed compulsion because it would involve the police. When the Bill was first introduced Lord R. Montagu asked: 'Who were to see that all the children attended school? Why, it would be necessary to have an army of inspectors as well as an army of police to see that the provisions of the Bill were properly carried out. Let them consider what an expense that alone would occasion to every locality.'[9]

The method adopted in the Act left it to the School Boards to make compulsory bye-laws if they thought fit and to appoint attendance officers if necessary. This policy of gradualism accustomed the people to the operation of the Act and also gave the School Boards power to fill the new schools they had built if attendance proved unsatisfactory. Some Radicals held the view that working men would welcome compulsion because they valued education, and enforcement would not be difficult. Compulsion had another advantage because it prevented the less reputable minority of parents from sending their children to work and undercutting the wages of more adult workers.

Religious instruction

> *Section 7.* Every public elementary school shall be conducted in accordance with the following regulations.

1. It shall not be required as a condition of any child being admitted into or continuing in the school, that he shall attend or abstain from attending any Sunday school, or any place of religious worship, or that he shall attend any religious observance or any instruction in religious subjects in the school or elsewhere or that he shall, if withdrawn by his parent, attend the school on any day exclusively set apart for religious observance by the religious body to which his parent belongs.
2. [Religious instruction] shall be either at the beginning or at the end or at the beginning and end of such meeting, and shall be inserted in a time table...
3. it shall be no part of the duties of such inspector to inquire into any instruction in religious subjects.

Section 14. .... 2. No religious catechism or religious formulary which is distinctive of any particular denomination shall be taught in the school (that is a school provided by a school board).

Section 97. 1. [The parliamentary grant] shall not be made in respect of any instruction in religious subjects; conditions shall not require that the school shall be in connexion with a religious denomination, or that religious instruction shall be given in the school, and shall not give any preference or advantage to any school on the ground that it is or is not provided by a school board.

One of the most difficult problems for the supporters of compulsory education was how to preserve the rights of conscience. The original Bill provided certain safeguards and allowed the School Boards to assist denominational schools out of the rates. As a Nonconformist, Mr Winterbotham protested against this 'because it will introduce religious strife worse than that of the Church rate, and it will lead, particularly in one-school parishes, to the Church school only being supported by a local rate'. It provided for the exemption of children from religious instruction on written objection by their parents. Mr Dixon, a Churchman, moved a resolution against this proposal because he thought the matter should be dealt with more in accordance with the expectations of the Nonconformists. Many of the poor would be unable to avail themselves of the protection afforded to religious liberty 'because of the influence of their superiors in social position'; he thought a timetable clause (see Section 7(2)) was the only practicable one. Professor Fawcett thought 'it was impossible to conceive a Conscience Clause more awkwardly devised than that provided by the Bill. It required that every rural labourer who wished to take advantage of the clause must make a request in writing to that effect. The chances were ten to one that he could not write. Nothing less, he ventured to think, would satisfy the Liberal party than the absolute separation of religious from secular teaching'.[10] Some were afraid there would be a contest for sectarian predominance in the School Boards, as the Bill allowed them to authorise religious instruction in their own schools. To this, Gladstone replied that the local rate payers must be left some discretion.

The result of these criticisms was a complete change in these clauses of the Bill: (a) the timetable conscience clause was introduced (proposed by Mr Cowper-Temple); (b) the denominational schools were separated from the School Boards and cut off from rate aid, and (c) in Board Schools denominational teaching was forbidden. This was the origin of the dual system which led to a rivalry between the Board Schools and the denominational schools and the decline of the latter. The only rate aid for denominational schools, if such it could be called, was the power of the School Board to pay for the free education of their necessitous children. This raised such violent protest that the law was changed in 1876 and the power passed to the Boards of Guardians. The Government gave increased grants to the denominational schools, as they were excluded from rate aid, but in the long run they had to turn to rate aid; this was authorised by the Act of 1902, by which time the Voluntary Schools were already on the decline.

The Radicals found a supporter in G. A. Trevelyan, who resigned from the Government because it had regarded too much the wishes of the Church of England and so prevented a great system of national education. John Bright thought the same: 'It was a Bill to encourage denominational education, and, where that was impossible, to establish Board Schools.' 'The fault of the Bill, in my mind,' he said, 'is that it has extended and confirmed the system which it ought in point of fact to have superseded.'[11] Cobden's friend Thorold Rogers denounced the Act as a 'pitiful compromise', and thought that educational policy should no longer be deferred 'to the professional interests of an established clergy, which is eager to maintain its ascendancy'.

Churchmen counterattacked with vigour. The Earl of Shaftesbury, at a meeting of the National Education Union, spoke of the secular policy as 'an outrage upon the national feelings, and more than this, it is without exception the grossest violation of the rights of religious liberty that was ever perpetrated, or even imagined, in the worst times by the bigotry of any Government whatever, foreign of domestic'.[12] Cowper-Temple, though he thought that the state should be unsectarian, yet insisted that it must be Christian and that some religious instruction should be compulsory. It seems that, with Gladstone, he did not think that his famous Conscience Clause would exclude the teaching of religious doctrines which were held in common by more than one sect. Lord Robert Montagu, speaking in 1872, referred to the 'classes to whom we have just given supreme political power; what prevented them from sending Proletaries or even Socialists and Internationalists as their Representatives to the House of Commons? Nothing but the respect for right which was in the breasts of the working classes—the traces of the religious teaching which they had received in the denominational schools of their youth. But bring up a new generation without religion, give them a habitual disregard and contempt for religion, and what would prevent them from looking merely to their own interests in the election of Members? They would then hurry in to the struggle between capital and labour. There would then be a Socialist House of Commons, which would speedily fall into contempt or worse—it would pass away and none would deplore it.'[13] In June *The Times* was afraid that the Bill might fail to pass because of the religious dissensions, but in summing up on 12 July said that 'denominationalism has, in fact, been put on a firmer basis'. Even so, Lord Ripon, the Lord President of the Council, had great difficulty in persuading the National Society to accept the Conscience Clause in some matters.

School Boards

Section 10. If after the expiration of a time not exceeding six months the education department are satisfied that all the public school accommodation required to be supplied has not been so supplied the education department shall cause a school board to be formed.

Section 12. In the following cases (that is to say)
1. Where application is made to the education department by the persons who, if there were a school board in that district, would elect the school board, or with respect to any borough, by the council;
2. Where the managers are unable or unwilling any longer to maintain such [elementary school] and if the school is discontinued, the amount of public school accommodation for such district will be insufficient, the education department may, if they think fit, cause a school board to be formed.

Section 54. Any sum required to meet any deficiency in the school fund shall be paid by the rating authority out of the local rate.

While the religious policy of the Act was closely defined and left little discretion to the administration, its social policy left the School Boards with wide permissive powers, and this displeased the Radicals. There was no universal compulsion and free education was to be very much the exception. Where there were no School Boards no provision was made in the Bill for free or compulsory education.

The creation of *ad hoc* School Boards followed the precedents of the Boards of Guardians, the Highway Boards, the Boards of Health and the Burial Boards. Apart from the municipal boroughs, some 220 all told, there was no comprehensive system of local government and even the boroughs were only slowly gaining a reputation for good administration. The first draft of the Bill provided for School Boards in areas where there was an educational deficiency and the municipal corporations and the vestries had the power to appoint the members of the Boards. This was opposed by the Nonconformists because it would give the Church an advantage. The Bill was then amended to substitute election by the ratepayers for nominations and to permit elections of School Boards even if there was no deficiency in school places. As a result, ninety-six School Boards were elected voluntarily in the boroughs, showing that there was no lack of enthusiasm for the tasks involved. In the country districts where Conservative feeling was strongest both the Church and the farmers were ready to take any steps to keep education off the rates.

It was inevitable that the powers given to the School Boards should be limited in scope since local government was not trusted in the nineteenth century. The bad administration which led to the municipal and Poor Law reforms in the 1830s was not easily forgotten and the governing powers in the counties lacked the vitality to cope with new problems. It was only to be expected that the new School Boards should be given a few powers and then, if they proved themselves worthy, the powers could be increased. If the Radicals had won the day it is quite likely that the administration of the School Boards would have failed to win public confidence, even as some say today that the planning powers of the Act of 1947 were too wide. There is a virtue in gradualism which enthusiasts too often overlook. The system before 1870 had created a teaching profession which was ready to undertake the new tasks, though we would consider that pupil teachers had too much work and that the classes were much too large. The encouragement given to school building had produced good results, though there were many places where new schools were needed. To many parents and children school attendance had become a matter of habit and the controls exercised over child labour had secured willing acceptance from the majority. It only remained to see if the School Boards would do their job properly, or if, like the Boards of Guardians, they would prove niggardly and inefficient. It is a tribute to the new spirit emerging in Victorian society at this time that the School Boards, in so many matters, triumphantly vindicated themselves.

Writing in 1886 Leslie Stephen expressed his doubts whether Forster could have moved more rapidly than he did in introducing so novel a principle as universal compulsion. He remarked that School Boards once set up would be likely to make the most of their permissive powers, as all official bodies had the vice of grasping as much power as possible. It was Auberon Herbert who recognised the evolutionary value of the Bill: 'It was with great pleasure he recognized in the Bill the principle of the School Board, the principle of a rate, and the principle of compulsion. He must also say that the principle of free schools—though they came into the Bill with a sort of apology for their place there—having once been seen on the blue paper of the Government Bill would never be lost sight of again.'[14]

> *Section 23.* The managers of any elementary school in the district of a school board may, in manner provided by this Act, make an arrangement with the school board for transferring their school to such school board, and the school board may assent to such arrangement.

This innocent-looking clause was effective in securing the extension of the powers of the School Boards over existing schools. Voluntary societies could never be certain that the income from local philanthropists would be regular enough to ensure the perpetual maintenance of their schools. With the increase in rates to build and manage the Board schools, some philanthropists would be sure to think twice about continuing their voluntary subscriptions. Lord Robert Montagu, at the first debate on the Education Bill of 1870, reminded Mr Forster 'that if he once allowed resort to a system of rates, numbers of persons would seek to evade the duty, which they now considered to be binding on them, that of supporting [voluntary] schools'. And later: 'they should embody in the Bill a clause exempting from the rates, to the amount of their subscriptions, those who supported an efficient school'. It was certain that as the cost of education increased and the old voluntary school buildings became more dilapidated and out of date the calls on the charitable would increase. The Board Schools also tended to be more up to date and to attract better teachers, so that the maintenance of the Voluntary Schools seemed less worth while. Many Nonconformist schools were handed over to the School Boards in the first ten years and subsequently more and more Church of England schools were surrendered. At least one Tory correctly foreshadowed the future: 'The effect of [the Bill] will be to do away with voluntary zeal, to do away with voluntary subscriptions, and speedily to annihilate the voluntary system.'[15] In the main, however, the religious societies hoped that in the period of grace before School Boards were formed, enough schools would be founded to ensure the unimportance of the Boards. They did not foresee that School Boards, by accepting lower school fees than the voluntary schools could afford to do, would undercut the latter and weaken their financial resources, while the longer pocket of the rate fund would enable the School Boards to improve their schools so long as they were not obsessed with saving the rates.

Criticism of the Act

To contemporaries the Act of 1870 was not a resounding success. One of the Inspectors wrote soon after it was passed: 'Many persons seem to think that buildings and teachers will secure efficient schools, but buildings and teachers are useless to children who do not attend, and only partially useful to those who attend irregularly, or even to those who attend regularly themselves, if others are allowed to attend irregularly, the irregular attendance of some keeping back the progress of all. The teachers struggle against the natural effects of this as much as they can; the regular attendants are kept back and the irregular pushed on: the classes are subdivided and the same ground gone over again, but the results are uniform; children discouraged, progress uncertain, apprentices [i.e. pupil teachers] perplexed, masters and mistresses disheartened, enthusiasm lost, and any high standard of excellency relinquished in utter despair.'[16] Even the teachers were criticised, and a circular of 1878 from the Education Department said: 'Their lordships have observed with great regret the large number of cases of falsification by teachers of the registers of attendance which have been brought to their notice.' In the same circular the school managers were also blamed for failure to exercise personal supervision over the schools and for not keeping in contact with the teachers and the children.

The disappointed Radicals were even more critical, and Mr Dixon proposed the following motion in the House in 1872: 'That in the opinion of this House, the provisions of the Elementary Education

Act are defective, and its working unsatisfactory; and particularly that it fails to secure the general election of School Boards in towns and rural districts; That it does not render obligatory the attendance of children at school; That it deals in a partial and irregular manner with the remission and payment of school fees by School Boards; That it allows the School Boards to pay fees out of rates levied upon the community, to denominational schools, over which the ratepayers have no control; That it permits School Boards to use the money of the ratepayers for the purpose of imparting dogmatic religious instruction in schools established by School Boards; That by the concession of these permissive powers it provokes religious discord throughout the country; and by the exercise of them it violates the rights of conscience.'[17] The Motion was lost by 94 to 355, but this Liberal minority of 94 had its revenge when Gladstone's government was defeated at the next election.

Thorold Rogers, friend and relative of Cobden, and co-author with Bright of Cobden's speeches, and Bright, were also critical. Cobden was particularly disappointed: 'Such a system of education [i.e. the pre 1870 voluntary system] could never become national in the true sense of the word, and despite its modifications under Mr Forster's Bill, never will be. It is either the business of the State or of the sects to teach secular knowledge. If it be the business of the State, the functions of the teacher of religion and the schoolmaster must be separated.'[18] To which he added that education left in the hands of the sects would be a failure because it would concentrate on proselytising. Adams in his book *The Elementary School Contest*, writing as a Nonconformist supporter, said: 'The Opposition to School Boards was led by the Bishops. The Bishop of Salisbury publicly returned thanks that there was only one School Board in an important part of his diocese. The Bishop of Hereford, with sly humour, told his clergy that "although the farmers might fear God, it could be taken for granted that they feared a rate more". '[19]

There were some optimists who hoped for better results in due course. Dr Lyon Playfair was not the only man in Parliament who hoped that there would be one Minister responsible for all aspects of education, though this was not achieved till the Act of 1899. In the more rarified atmosphere of the Social Science Association he spoke of the need for secondary and even university education for some of the pupils of primary schools and gave as an example the schemes which were to be found in Scotland and Germany. In this he was supported by G. W. Hastings, Dr Dudley Field (an American), and Mr Bourne. Sir Alexander Grant, a Minister for Education in India, said: 'The first privilege and right of a man, to which he was born, consisted in his reception of education, but not some wretched modicum that must keep him in the lower ranks. Every man ought to enjoy the privilege of fully developing his mind.' He opposed the idea of state education as a form of intellectual outdoor relief. 'If they could only get rid of the notion that primary schools must be restricted to the lowest and most meagre elements of education, then they might start altogether upon a new career.'[20]

In such a welter of opinions the Education Act of 1870 started on its way with very limited objectives. To later generations it might have seemed to be the beginning of socialism, although it was based in the main on the ideas of individualism. No one said it was a leap in the dark like the Reform Act of 1867, and yet its consequences were even less foreseen than the extension of the franchise. To Dr E. G. West,[21] and to those who think that a national scheme of state education is fundamentally unnecessary, it was no doubt the beginning of state paternalism and a usurpation of the right of free choice in education, but this is a comparatively new idea. The most uncertain part of the Act seemed to contemporaries to be the religious settlement and yet, in general, this survived until 1944. Politicians know not what they build and the foundations of 1870 were strong enough for a super-structure which to Gladstone and his men would have seemed like a mighty tower and a monument to national extravagance could they have lived for the next hundred years.

REFERENCES

1. Hans. 17 Feb. 1870, vol. 199. c. 443.
2. Hans. 1 July 1870, vol. 202, c. 1312; free secondary education came in 1944.
3. Hans. 22 July 1870, vol. 203, c. 747.
4. Hans. 18 Mar. 1870, vol. 200, c. 262.
5. PP 1870, vol. 26, p. 444.
6. Hans. 18 Mar. 1870, vol. 200, c. 298.
7. Hans. 8 July 1970, vol. 202, c. 1745–6.
8. Hans. 18 Mar. 1870, vol. 200, c. 235.
9. Hans. 17 Feb. 1870. vol. 199, c. 474.
10. Hans. 18 Mar. 1870, vol. 200, c. 280–1.
11. Public Addresses by John Bright, ed., Thorold Rogers, p. 201 (speaking on 22 Oct. 1873).
12. Edwin Hodder, *Lord Shaftesbury*, p. 644 (popular edn.).
13. Hans. 5 Mar. 1872, vol. 209, c. 1453–4.
14. Hans. 15 Mar. 1870, Vol. 199, c. 2051.

8

15. Hans. 18 Mar. 1870, vol. 200, c. 259, Col. Beresford.
16. PP 1871, vol. 22, p. 22.
17. Hans. 5 Mar. 1872, vol. 209, c. 1395.
18. Thorold Rogers, *Cobden and Political Opinion*, p. 349 (speaking in 1873).
19. F. Adams, *The Elementary School Contest*, p. 242.
20. TNAPSS 1870, pp. 318–19.
21. E. G. West, *Education and the State*. 1965.

8

The Harvest—1870 to 1970

Compulsory education

Have we advanced so far in the hundred years since 1870 that the issues which were then discussed are no longer relevant? Can we say that the conflict of ideas which produced so much turmoil among our grandfathers has been entirely resolved? The tentative proposals about compulsory attendance for children aged five to thirteen have now taken a new form in the suggestions for compulsory attendance at County Colleges in the Act of 1944 and for extending the leaving age to sixteen. Free education now applies to secondary education as well as elementary education. The universities are receiving government grants in much the same way as the schools were aided in the years 1833–70. It is still a problem to determine what fees should be charged at institutions of higher education and at what point a means test should be applied. The religious settlement of the Act of 1944 is still challenged by the secularists and humanists of today, while the value of education without a religious backing in reducing crime, pauperism and strikes, as well as educating voters, is still a subject for argument. The Act of 1870 provided a temporary solution to some of these problems and the foundations which it laid have proved stronger than some of the Radicals of the time prophesied. Other historical changes such as the depreciation in the value of money which brought the Voluntary Schools nearer bankruptcy, the growth of more socialistic ideas and the development of secondary and higher education modified the administration of the Act of 1870 and led to new legislation expanding its influence. If some of the ideas of Members of Parliament in 1870, such as education to maintain social status, seem now to be unimportant, nevertheless the proposals for comprehensive schools and the future of public schools is essentially the unresolved problem of social status and the quality of state education.

Political and philosophical questions concerning the freedom of the child and of the parent, the right to choose a denominational school, the limits to be placed on the employment of children, the right to free education, free books, free meals at school and free journeys to school, these are questions which are still alive today and may not be fully resolved one hundred years hence. If in our own generation we can build on as firm foundations as those built in 1870 we need not be ashamed. The greatest danger is from enthusiasts who would make laws which are not enforceable because the state lacks the means to carry them out, or because public opinion is not ripe for the exercise of new powers. It would have been better if the Day Continuation Schools of 1918 had been left in the administrator's 'pending basket'; yet despite this example, the Act of 1944 provided for county colleges which have still to come to life. They might have been useful to absorb the unemployment which some expected to follow the war of 1939–45, but if there had been such an economic crisis, would not a campaign of economy have killed them as the Day Continuation Schools were killed in the years between 1919 and 1922?

The most important new principles of the Act of 1870 was that of compulsory education. It had found a place in the Factory Acts of 1833–67, but at the most less than 100,000 school places were filled in this way in 1870, though they rose to over 200,000 before the Act of 1880, and the number was still above 175,000 before the Act of 1893 made eleven the minimum age for such employment. There was a burst of enthusiasm for part-time education of factory children about 1860, but the Inspectors on the whole did not find it satisfactory. The compulsory principle as embodied in the Act of 1870 was only a permissive power given to School Boards; even so the Liberal Vernon Harcourt said in 1873 that 'the doctrine of compulsion had not found favour with the people of this country. Even for the greatest public objects, such as that of national defence, the English people had never been willing to accept the doctrine of compulsory service.'[1] Where there were no School Boards there was no power of compulsion until the Act of 1876 gave permissive powers to newly created bodies called School Attendance Committees. In 1880 an Act was passed requiring all such authorities to make compulsory attendance bye-laws so that in due course the whole country was covered, but it must be realised that even after that date the average attendance was poor. The Department of Education had to use its statutory powers to compel the election of School Boards in over 1,100 areas out of a total of 2,545 in England and Wales. The Boards covered a total population of twenty million in the year 1900 and at the same date there were 788 School Attendance Committees in areas with a total population of nearly nine million. The School Attendance Committees were mainly found in the rural and semi-rural areas. One Inspector in his report of 1901 says: 'A rural district provides unusual opportunities for the habitual irregularity of both boys and girls, which is encouraged by the no secret knowledge that the authorities will take no notice of children who attend about seven or eight of the ten weekly meetings. There have been in this district [outside Colchester] scores of children who never made ten weekly attendances and this is the worst kind of irregularity. Until the attendance question is put into other than local hands, the working of the compulsory clauses of the Education Act will continue to be unsatisfactory.'[2] In another report of the same year the writer says: 'The individual members of these [attendance] committees too often fear their electors and it is not unknown for a magistrate to calculate the effect on the rates of sending a child to an industrial school [the ultimate legal sanction for bad attendance] and, by his estimate, influencing the judgment of his brethren on the bench.'[3] Sometimes the committees blamed the teachers for irregular attendances because they sent children home who failed to bring the school fees.

Compulsion under the Education Act was applied to achieve a beneficial social objective and not, as in previous legislation, to apply a principle of protection to those in danger of abuse by their employers or of neglect by public authorities. But compulsory bye-laws infringed the liberty of the parent, particularly in the employment of his children, as some politicians were not slow to point out. Yet compulsory school attendance was made a condition of outdoor poor relief by an Act of 1873. The Act of 1876 declared that it was the duty of the parent to cause his child to receive efficient elementary instruction and prohibited the employment of children under ten (eight in agricultural areas if the authority saw fit); so long as the child was not employed under the age of fourteen the duty was not enforced by legal penalties, unless the local authority had made attendance bye-laws which at that time covered about 50 per cent of the child population. The only other sanction to enforce the duty under the Act of 1876 was the need for an educational certificate of proficiency in reading, writing and elementary arithmetic or of attendance at a certified efficient school before a child aged ten to fourteen could be employed. Such exemptions, known as the dunces certificate, continued till 1918, though the minimum age of ten was raised ultimately to thirteen. The Act also provided for the enforcement of School Attendance Orders against defaulting parents or children wandering and not under proper control. Even in 1880, when some 73 per cent were subject to attendance bye-laws, the age limits for compulsory attendance were only five to ten (or eight in some agricultural areas) for the country as a whole, but the more advanced authorities had the power to fix the limits at five to thirteen, subject to certain exceptions. The exceptions were contained in clauses of the Factory, etc. Acts and not until the Act of 1918, when there were some 70,000 half-time children, mostly employed in agriculture, was the part-time employment under these Acts abolished and made subordinate to the general law of school attendance. The minimum age of ten had been raised to eleven in 1893 and twelve in 1899 (with exceptions for agricultural areas), but in 1914 40 per cent of children left school before reaching the age of fourteen. The Act of 1918 made fourteen the minimum school leaving age, although local authorities could fix the limit at fifteen. The general school leaving age was fixed at fifteen in 1947; this may be raised to sixteen shortly when there are sufficient school places and teachers and the campaign for public economy is relaxed.

Free education

The Act of 1870 only gave a partial recognition to the idea of free education, and even the Radical Mr Fawcett, Professor of Political Economy at Cambridge, who supported compulsory education, condemned the principle because it would lead to a general system of free education: 'It should not be forgotten that free education was the first plank in the programme of the International.' School Boards could provide free schools in slum areas and the school fees of children of poor parents could be paid by the board even for the children attending Voluntary Schools, where free education for all was only achieved by the Act of 1918. The Education Code of 1901 still required that in elementary schools the maximum fee should be 9d per week and that not more than one-third of the scholars should pay this maximum fee. The writer well remembers clutching the school pence in his hand on Monday mornings and hurrying past the sweet shop with one last long lingering look behind while fleeing from temptation. One M.P. complained in 1875 that the School Boards 'by reducing their own fee, undermine and take away the children from Voluntary Schools. He thought the government ought to give earnest attention to this grievance, so that the voluntary system, which was generally growing, should at least have a fair field and no favour.'[4] The Voluntary Schools were required by the Code under which they earned government grants to raise a minimum part of their income from voluntary subscriptions and school fees. In 1891 an Act gave the parents the right to free education in Boards Schools, and although the

Voluntary Schools received extra grants in compensation, they felt the pinch. By 1902 only 633,000 paid fees and over five million children had free education. In the thirty years following the Act of 1870, 1,372 Voluntary Schools were transferred to School Boards, of which 973 were Church of England schools, 24 Wesleyan and 271 British and Foreign School Society. By 1940 the number of Church of England schools had fallen to 9,000 from their peak of 14,000 before 1900 and they taught only 22 per cent of the elementary school population. The policy of free education was extended to secondary schools by the Act of 1944, but it did not apply to direct grant schools, and this has raised a thorny problem of social status. The means test is still used in deciding whether to grant free school meals and in assessing fees for certain forms of higher education, so that the educational expenses of the needy still hamper the educational administrator, though there is no suggestion of pauperism which bedevilled the arguments of 1870.

Voluntary Schools

The most marked change in the years since 1870 has been the decline of the Voluntary Schools, the Roman Catholic schools excepted. With the increase in national taxation and local rates there has been less money willingly available for Voluntary Schools attended by children of the working classes. Both inflation and the increasing cost of running schools, because of higher standards of education, have left the voluntary bodies with more money to find. The Board Schools set the pace with better school buildings and equipment and higher rates of pay for teachers, because their financial resources were better. In the debates of 1870 Forster had prophesied a maximum rate of 3*d*, but by 1880 the London rate was already over 5*d*, Birmingham over 6*d* and Leeds over 7*d*. When ratepayers found the rates going up it was not unexpected that their charitable contributions to Church schools declined. The fee income of these schools did not suffer and it was even rising in the year 1900, but the cause was no doubt the social segregation which pleased some better off parents who were anxious to avoid sending their children to the 'slum schools'. For many years there were more headships available for teachers in Voluntary Schools and the denominational training colleges had the field to themselves. Even in 1902 there were less than 6,000 Board Schools but over 14,000 Voluntary Schools. But usually the School Boards were able to offer better-paid positions, mostly in larger schools, and the attraction of the Church schools to the teaching profession was not so great. To be under the thumb of the parson and the squire in a small village could sometimes be very irksome. New secular training colleges run by the local authorities, now numbering two-thirds of all such colleges, were developed after 1890; they raised up a class of teachers who were less interested in religious instruction, so that from all sides the denominational schools suffered, even though they qualified for more financial aid by the Acts of 1902, 1936, 1944 and 1959.

Only a handful of M.P.s in 1870 wished for strictly secular education and the majority willingly accepted the compromise of unsectarian religious teaching. By 1894 only fifty School Boards in Wales and seven in England adopted a secular policy. The religious settlement of 1870 certainly seemed fragile (like the French constitution of 1875–1946) but it lasted until 1944, apart from the increase of government grants to Voluntary Schools and the subsequent assistance from the rates. The secularists of 1870 would have been surprised by the settlement of 1944: 'the school day in every county school and in every voluntary school shall begin with collective worship on the part of all pupils in attendance'; and 'religious instruction shall be given in every county school and every voluntary school'.[5] The freedom of the parent to withdraw his child was of course given legal guarantee as in 1870, but the timetable section of the Cowper-Temple clause of 1870, which seemed to have become a permanent part of the legal and religious settlement, was jettisoned, though the phrase which excludes teaching 'distinctive of any particular [religious] denomination' finds its place in the 1944 Act. There were many months of negotiation in 1942 and 1943 with the religious bodies to achieve the desired result, but there was no such public commotion as in 1870. Perhaps in 1943–4 the war had diverted the attention of the public, or even made them more religious-minded for a time, but it was a surprising settlement in a century which has shown a growing indifference to church attendance.

Some Radical critics of the establishment in the years before 1870 said the Tories only wanted religious education for the poor to teach them submission, and showed no special care for it in the education of their own children. The Act of 1944, however, does apply to the former grammar schools where middle-class children were taught, so that the secularists of today could no longer make this complaint, but technical colleges are not covered by this section of the Act.

Higher education

The period from 1850 marks a growing interest by the state in secondary and higher education. The universities were the subject of investigation and reform, and so were the major public schools. The other secondary schools were made subject under the Endowed Schools Act of 1869 to the Charity Commissioners (from 1874) but there was no vast expansion of secondary education, despite the complaints of some politicians that the education of the middle classes was being neglected. The cry of over-education was raised in the House in 1876 by Mr Sandford, who 'considered it a most dangerous thing to convert a nation of labourers into a nation of clerks. There was no greater proof of the decay of a country than when its inhabitants despised manual labour.'[6] The Act of 1870 did not apply to secondary schools, but because it did not define elementary education in scholastic terms, it was possible for some of the more advanced School Boards to develop Higher Grade or Higher Elementary schools. Here secondary education was given with the knowledge and agreement of the Education Department. The support which parents gave to these schools showed that there was an unsatisfied demand for secondary education; in 1913–14 over 47,000 children over age fourteen were attending elementary schools. The Technical Instruction Act of 1889 gave powers to the newly created county and county borough councils to deal with somewhat similar work and they claimed that the School Boards were exceeding their functions. They also raised objection to Boards running night schools as these were not mentioned in any of the Acts, though they were recognised under the Code and received considerable financial help from the Department of Science and Art. From 1880 School Boards were certainly within their powers in running pupil teacher's centres to train the young apprentices before they were admitted to the training colleges and these centres were certainly comparable with secondary schools in their scope. The money spent by the School Boards on Higher Elementary schools was the subject of a test case and in the Cockerton judgment (1900) such expenditure was declared illegal. This legal decision was one reason for the Education Act of 1902 which abolished the School Boards and transferred all their powers to some of the existing local authorities, but secondary and technical education was a function of the counties and county boroughs only. Thus the expansion of secondary education was in no small part due to the Act of 1870.

Progress and development

During the debates on the Bill of 1902 the School Boards fought hard for their lives against the new local authorities and judged by their

9

achievements they had a good case, but it was necessary for administration to be simplified. Although religious dissensions hampered some of the Boards they generally resolved their problems satisfactorily. School buildings, school attendance and the quality of teaching had improved a good deal by 1902. In London the average size of a class per adult teacher had been reduced from about eighty-five to forty-two, but the national average was much higher. In England and Wales the number of certificated teachers had risen from under 3,000 in 1855 to nearly 14,000 in 1870, to more than 62,000 by 1900 and to 129,000 by 1933. The average attendance was 70 per cent in 1880 and reached 87 per cent for older scholars by 1900. But even in 1902 there were more than 20,000 prosecutions for bad attendance in London alone. When it is remembered how niggardly was the policy of the Boards of Guardians in this period, it is surprising that the School Boards showed themselves so venturesome, though a few in the country districts limited their powers to a minimum. The prophesy made by Lord Robert Montagu in 1870 was not fulfilled: 'They would soon see the same result in England as had been brought about in Canada and in America; the system would be administered as cheaply as possible, and education would be greatly deteriorated.'[7] The Education Department (Board of Education from 1899) and Her Majesty's Inspectors played an important part in encouraging the School Boards to carry out their duties and to stimulate them where they showed signs of negligence, but the triumph of these thirty years must go in large part to the enthusiasm of the School Boards throughout the country.

The Act of 1902 abolished some 2,500 School Boards and nearly 800 School Attendance Committees and transferred the responsibility for supervising the work of some 14,000 Voluntary School managers from the Education Department to the 328 local education authorities. The new authorities proved their worth in the years which followed and the Board of Education was able to deal with the larger issues and plan the line of advance. Many Nonconformists, under the leadership of Dr Clifford, with support from Lloyd George, protested strongly against the Act of 1902, claiming that it put religion on the rates because the local authorities had to give rate aid to Voluntary Schools, but by 1910 his passive resistance movement was dead, although at first some 70,000 Nonconformists were prosecuted for refusal to pay the rate. In one houshold, known to the writer, the minister every half year surrendered his silver teapot for non-payment of the rate and it was bought back by a faithful supporter and returned to the minister ready for the next half year; this went on for some six or seven years

Dr Clifford was again on the war-path in 1919–20, but his agitation was less successful.

The fringe developments of the education service, such as school meals, school medical service and special schools for those who could not be educated in ordinary schools, were not foreshadowed in the 1870 Act, but they arose directly out of the experience of teachers and administrators; yet even in 1871 an Education of the Blind Bill was introduced, though it did not pass its second reading. It was difficult enough in the early days to get children to attend, but once this had been achieved, particularly after the Act of 1891 opened the door to free education, it was possible to concentrate on the best possible means of seeing that the educational benefits were available to all children, the bright and the stupid, the badly fed and the well fed, the sick and the maimed. For a time it seemed possible that Forster would exclude children under four from qualifying for the grant, but he met with such resistance on the grounds that such children were better at school and partly because older children would be kept at home to mind them, that he relented, so that children of three years of age could earn the grant so long as they were four by the day of inspection.

The progressive improvement of standards in buildings, in teaching and in equipment belongs to the present century, but the really hard task of laying the foundations fell upon those who in the slum areas of our great towns must have been inspired by an enthusiasm equal to that of the prophets of a new religion and for them the Act of 1870 was a corner stone in the building of a new world. Today the education of the people is a matter of public concern and the main problem is how to raise the money for the service and how to spend it to the best advantage. In the struggle for the Act of 1870 the fundamental principles were debated and from the Act itself has sprung many social and educational services which are in operation today.

REFERENCES

1. Hans. 22 July 1873, vol. 217, c. 756.
2. PP 1901, vol. 19, vol 2, p. 7.
3. PP 1901, vol. 19, vol. 2, p. 38
4. Hans. 9 June 1875, vol. 224, c. 1581.
5. Education Act 1944, Section 25.
6. Hans. 5 Apr. 1876, vol. 228, c. 1269.
7. Hans. 17 Feb. 1870, vol. 199, c. 473.

Bibliography

Primary sources

(*a*) Official papers, debates, periodicals
Parliamentary Papers (abbr. PP).
Hansard's *Parliamentary Debates* (abbr. Hans.).
The Annual Register.
The Times.
Transactions of the National Association for the Promotion of Social Science
(abbr. TNAPSS).
Board of Education—Education Miscellanies.

(*b*) Histories, essays, novels, biographies, etc.
ADAMS, F. *The Elementary School Contest.* 1882.
BRIGHT, JOHN. *Speeches.* 1868.
BRIGHT, JOHN. *Public Letters.* 1885.
BRIGHT, JOHN. *Public Addresses*, ed. Thorold Rogers. 1879.
CARLYLE, T. *Essays.* 1872.
COBDEN, RICHARD. *Speeches on Questions of Public Policy*, ed. J. Bright
and Thorold Rogers. 1870.
Crosby Hall Lectures, (publd. John Snow, London, 1848).
DISRAELI, BENJAMIN. *Sybil.* 1845.
FAWCETT, HENRY. *Essays and Lectures.* 1872.
GATHORNE-HARDY, A. E. (1st Earl Cranbrook). *A Memoir*, 1910.
GREEN, J. R. *Letters*, ed. Leslie Stephen. 1901.
HOBHOUSE, L. T. and HAMMOND, S. L. *Lord Hobhouse : A Memoir.* 1905.
HODDER, EDWIN. *Samuel Morley.* 1887.
HODDER, EDWIN. *Lord Shaftesbury.* Popular edn. 1887.
KAY-SHUTTLEWORTH, J. *Four Periods of English Education.* 1862.
KAY-SHUTTLEWORTH, J. *Public Education.* 1853.
KINGSLEY, CHARLES. *Yeast.* 1848.
KINGSLEY, CHARLES. *Alton Locke*, 1850 (1876 edn.).
LOVETT, WILLIAM. *Autobiography.* Trübner, 1876.

MARTINEAU, HARRIET. *History of England during the Thirty Years' Peace, 1816–1846.* 1849 (1877 edn.).

MILL, J. S. *Autobiography,* 1873. ed. H. J. Laski. Worlds Classics edn., 1924.

MILL, J. S. *Letters,* ed. H. S. R. Elliot. Longmans, 1910.

MILL, J. S. *On Liberty.* 1859. Worlds Classics edn., 1901.

MONYPENNY, W. F. and BUCKLE, G. E. *Life of Benjamin Disraeli,* 6 vols. 1910–18.

PARKER, C. S. *Sir James Graham.* 1907.

PARKER, C. S. *Sir Robert Peel.* 1899.

REID, T. WEMYSS. *W. E. Forster.* 1888.

The Sea Board and the Down, by an Old Vicar. 1860.

Secondary sources

ADAMSON, J. W. *English Education 1789 to 1902.* Cambridge U.P., 1965.

BAGEHOT, W. *Works and Life.* Longmans, 1915.

BALFOUR, GRAHAM. *Educational Systems of Great Britain and Ireland,* 2nd edn. Oxford U.P., 1903.

BEER, M. *History of British Socialism.* Allen & Unwin, 1940.

BINNS, H. B. *A Century of Education.* 1908.

BIRCHENOUGH, C. *History of Elementary Education in England and Wales from 1800 to the Present Day.* 1st edn. University Tutorial Press, 1914.

BREADY, J. WESLEY. *Lord Shaftesbury.* Allen & Unwin, 1926.

BROWN, C. K. FRANCIS. *The Church's Part in Education, 1833–1941.* S.P.C.K., 1942.

BROWN, P. A. *The French Revolution in English History.* C. Lockwood, 1918.

CANNON, C. 'The influence of religion on educational policy', *British Journal of Educational Studies.* 1964.

CONNELL, W. F. *Educational Thought and Influences of Matthew Arnold.* Routledge & Kegan Paul, 1950.

CORNISH, F. WARRE. *History of the English Church in the Nineteenth Century.* 1910.

CRAIK, SIR HENRY. *Education.* 1896.

CRUICKSHANK, M. *Church and State in English Education 1870–1962.* Macmillan, 1963.

DARK, SIDNEY. *Archbishop Davidson and the English Church.* P. Allan, 1929.

DICEY, A. V. *Lectures on the Relation between Law and Public Opinion in England,* 2nd edn. Macmillan, 1919.

DOBBS, A. E. *Education and Social Movements 1700–1850.* Longmans, 1919.

DUNLOP, O. J. and DENMAN, R. D. *English Apprenticeship and Child Labour.* 1912.

FEARON, D. *School Inspector : 1860–1870.* 1876.

GOSDEN, P. H. J. H. *Development of Educational Administration in England and Wales.* Blackwell, 1966.

GREEN, T. H. *Collected Works,* 2nd edn., ed. R. L. Nettleship. 1890.

GREGORY, DEAN. *Elementary Education.* 1895.

GWYNN, DENIS. *A Hundred Years of Catholic Emancipation.* Longmans, 1929.

GWYNNE, S. and TUCKWELL, G. M. *Life of Dilke.* John Murray, 1917.

HOLMAN, H. *English National Education,* 1898.

HUTCHINS, B. L. and HARRISON, A. *History of Factory Legislation,* 3rd edn. P. S. King, 1926.

HUMPHREYS, A. W. *Robert Applegarth, Trade Unionist, Educationalist, Reformer.* Manchester, 1913.

LINDSAY, K. *Social Progress and Educational Waste.* Routledge & Kegan Paul, 1926.

MARSTON, M. *Sir Edwin Chadwick.* Leonard Parsons, 1925.

MONTMORENCY, J. E. G. DE (Lord Gorell). *State Intervention in English Education.* 1902.

MORLEY, JOHN. *Life of Gladstone.* 1903.

MURRAY, R. H. *Social and Political Thinkers of the Nineteenth Century,* 2 vols. W. Heffer, 1929.

PORTER, C. R. *Progress of the Nation in Social and Economic Relations,* ed. Hirst. Methuen (1912 edn.).

RAVEN, C. E. *Christian Socialism.* Macmillan, 1920.

RICH, R. W. *The Training of Teachers in England and Wales.* Cambridge U.P., 1933.

ROBSON, A. H. *The Education of Children Engaged in Industry, 1833–76.* Routledge & Kegan Paul. 1931

ROGERS, THOROLD. *Cobden and Political Opinion.* 1873.

REDFORD, A. *Labour Migration in England 1800–1850.* Manchester U.P. 1926.

SELBIE, W. B. *Nonconformity.* Home Univ. Library, 1912.

SIMON, BRIAN. *Studies in the History of Education, 1780–1870.* Lawrence & Wishart, 1960.

SMITH, FRANK. *A History of English Elementary Education, 1760–1902.* University of London Press, 1931.

SMITH, FRANK. *Life and Work of Sir James Kay-Shuttleworth.* John Murray 1923.

STEPHEN, LESLIE. *Life of Henry Fawcett.* 1886.

STEWART, H. L. *A Century of Anglo-Catholicism.* Dent, 1929.

STURT, MARY. *The Education of the People*. Routledge & Kegan Paul, 1967.

SZRETER, R. 'Origins of "Age 5" ', *British Journal of Educational Studies*, 1964.

WAGNER D. O. *The Church of England and Social Reform since 1854*. Columbia University Studies in History, P. S. King, 1930.

WEST, E. G. 'Education and the State', *Institute of Economic Affairs*, 1965.

Biographical Index

Adderley, Sir Charles Bowyer (1st Baron Norton), 1814–1905. M.P. 1841–78. A landowner of evangelical views though a strong churchman. A liberal-minded Tory, with friends in both political parties. Vice-President of the Committee of Privy Council on Education 1858–9. Took an active interest in social and educational reforms and sponsored more than one education bill. See pages 27, 94, 95.

Baines, Sir Edward, 1800–90. Liberal M.P. 1859–74. Editor of the *Leeds Mercury* (following his father, also Edward Baines, M.P. 1834–41). He was a leading Congregationalist and a student of sociology and economics. Leader of the Voluntaryist party 1843–67. Member of the Schools Inquiry Commission (Endowed Schools) 1865. See pages 34–6, 50, 68, 80.

Bright, John, 1811–89. Liberal M.P. for most of the period 1843–86. A Quaker. Son of a cotton mill owner and later a partner. A radical supporter of social reforms but unsympathetic to state education (in 1847), to factory legislation, and to the landed aristocracy. One of the leaders of the Anti-Corn Law League. A member of Gladstone's government 1868–70 but ill from January 1870. In 1873 attacked the denominational character of the Education Act 1870. See pages 97, 102.

Brougham, Henry Peter (Lord Brougham) 1778–1868. Whig M.P. for most of the period 1810–31. Active in the cause of education from 1816. Published *Observations on the education of the people*, 1825. Founder of London University 1828. See pages 24, 28, 75, 81.

Chadwick, Edwin, 1800–90. Disciple of Jeremy Bentham. Trained as a lawyer and an ardent advocate of legal reform particularly of the Poor Laws and the Factory Laws; also worked for sanitary reforms and to a lesser degree for educational improvements. For many years a leading public official and a successful but over zealous administrator. See pages 49, 63, 70.

Cobden, Richard, 1804–65. Liberal M.P. for most of the years 1841–65. Leader of the Anti-Corn Law League. A partner in a cotton trading firm. A middle-class radical with strong social sympathies for the poor, but this did not extend to factory legislation or the strengthening of the trade unions. Advocated educational reforms. See pages 20, 58, 78, 79–80, 81, 97, 102.

Cowper, William Francis, afterwards Cowper-Temple (later Lord Mount-Temple), 1811–88. M.P. 1835–80. First Vice-President of the Committee of Privy Council on Education 1857–58. Author of the Cowper-Temple clause in the Education Act 1870. See pages 51, 97–8.

Denison, George Anthony, 1805–96. Archdeacon of Taunton. A leading and vigorous controversialist of the High Church group. Brother of J. E. Denison, Speaker of the House of Commons 1857–82, who was the author of Denison's Act 1855 on the education of pauper children. See pages 32, 37, 42.

Dilke, Sir Charles Wentworth, 1843–1911. Radical M.P. 1868–86. Opposed the Education Bill of 1870; he successfully moved an amendment to secure directly elected school boards. See page 94.

Dixon, George, 1820–98. An advanced Liberal M.P. 1867–76 and 1885–98. Advocate of compulsory state education. First President of the National Education League. Member of Birmingham School Board 1870–97. See pages 96, 101.

Fawcett, Henry, 1833–84. M.P. 1865–84. Belonged to the circle of friends of John Stuart Mill. A member of the radicals in Parliament and a critic of the Education Bill 1870. Professor of Political Economy at Cambridge. See pages 76, 84, 86, 92, 96, 108.

Forster, William Edward, 1818–86. M.P. 1861–86. A Quaker in his youth. At one time engaged in the woollen trade. An advanced Liberal and the Minister responsible for the Education Bill of 1870. See pages 48, Chap. 7, 113.

Fox, William Johnson, 1786–1864. M.P. 1847–63. A nonconformist Minister who became a Unitarian; preacher and journalist. Friend of Forster and John Stuart Mill. Sponsored the Secular Education Bill of 1850; a member of the National Public Schools Association. See pages 26–7, 68, 69, 70, 75.

Gladstone, William Ewart, 1809–98. M.P. for most of the time from 1832. Strongly attached to the Church of England. A member of Peel's Tory ministry of 1841–46, but became leader of the Liberal party in the Commons, 1866. Prime Minister 1868–74 and later. In educational matters he was right of centre. See pages 38, 41, 45, 79, 81, 90, 93, 97, 98, 103.

Graham, Sir James Robert George, 1792–1868. M.P. 1818–21 and from 1826. At first a Whig but from 1835 a supporter of Peel. Home Secretary 1841–6 and responsible for the Factory Bill of 1843. See pages 31, 58, 74, 83.

Henley, Joseph Warner, 1793–1884. M.P. 1841–78. A Tory and a strong Churchman. See pages 26, 48, 58, 76.

Hook, Walter Farquhar, 1798–1875. Vicar of Leeds; from 1859 Dean of Chichester. An independently minded clergyman of reforming views though inclined in some matters to High Church theories. His letter of 1846 on a scheme for national education providing for all religious denominations was widely circulated. See pages 42, 74, 82.

Hume, Joseph, 1777–1855. M.P. for much of the period 1812–55. For many years the leader of the Radicals. An active member of the Royal Lancastrian Society. See pages 40, 47–8, 68, 76, 79.

Inglis, Sir Robert Harry, 1776–1855. M.P. for Oxford University 1829–54, but sat for broken periods 1824–9. A Tory politician and a strong Churchman. See pages 31, 79.

Kay-Shuttleworth, Sir James Phillips (originally Dr Kay), 1804–77. Secretary to the Manchester Board of Health. Assistant Poor Law Commissioner 1835, where he first showed his interest in education. First Secretary of the Committee of Privy Council on Education 1839 to 1849. Joint founder of Battersea Teachers' Training College 1840. Continued to write trenchantly on education after 1849. His son Ughtred spoke in the Commons' debates on the Bill of 1870. See pages 17, 23, 29, 32, 51, 55, 59, 61, 64, 74, 79, 83–4.

Kingsley, Charles, 1819–75. Clergyman and novelist. A leading member of the 'Christian Socialist' group, which aimed at improving social conditions following the collapse of Chartism. Opposed the High Church movement though he was no radical in politics. Strong sympathies towards children. He joined the National Education League but later withdrew to support the Education Bill of 1870. See pages 45, 53, 54, 82.

Lowe, Robert, 1811–92. M.P. 1852–80 when he was made 1st Viscount Sherbrooke. Vice-President of the Committee of Council on Education 1859–64. under the Whig Government; author of the Revised Code, 'payment by results', 1861–2. In the debates on electoral reform in 1867 he used words which have since been summarised as 'We must educate our masters'. See pages 14, 18, 40, 60, 67, 68, 70, 80.

Miall, Edward, 1809–81. M.P. 1852–7 and 1869–74. A Nonconformist minister who favoured the disestablishment of the Church of England. A Voluntaryist. Member of the Newcastle Commission 1858–61. See pages 33, 36.

Mill, John Stuart, 1806–73. M.P. 1865–8. Political philosopher and economist. Deeply interested in social problems and had considerable influence among a wide circle of political friends. In Parliament he supported Gladstone. Though he urged the need for more education of the people he was critical of education by the state. See pages 5, 9, 26, 47, 82, 83, 84.

Montagu, Lord Robert, 1825–1902. Conservative M.P. 1859–80 of strong High Church views but supported the conscience clause when he was Vice-President 1867–8; he was critical of the Bill of 1870. See pages 28, 95, 98, 100, 112.

Mundella, Anthony John, 1825–97. M.P. 1868–97 with Radical views. A hosiery manufacturer who played a prominent part in the passing of the Factories Act 1874. Vice-President of the Committee of Privy Council on Education 1880–5, and responsible for the Education Act 1880 (often known as the Mundella Act) requiring compulsory attendance bye-laws in all areas. See page 106.

Northcote, Sir Stafford Henry (1st Earl of Iddesleigh, cr. 1885) 1818–87. M.P. for most of the period 1855–85. Conservative politician. A secretary to Mr Gladstone in the 1840s. Advocated reform of the Civil Service. Was interested in Reformatory and Industrial Schools. See pages 47, 58.

Pakington, Sir John Somerset (1st Baron Hampton), 1799–1880. Conservative M.P. 1837–74. A frequent speaker on education in Parliament who proposed the motion leading to the appointment of the Newcastle Commission in 1858. He introduced an unsuccessful Education Bill in 1855. See pages 28, 67, 69, 75, 92.

Peel, Sir Robert, 1788–1850. M.P. 1809–50. His father owned a Lancashire cotton factory and was responsible for the Act of 1802 which eased the lot of pauper apprentices. Peel was a Tory who was converted to free trade ideas. Prime Minister in 1834 and 1841–6. In 1846 the right wing members of this party broke away from his leadership. See pages 25, 30, 31, 37, 45, 67, 69.

Roebuck, John Arthur. 1801–79. M.P. for most of the period 1832–79. An independent member of the Commons with reformist views. Introduced a motion on Education in 1833 and though it failed it was followed soon after by the first government grant on education. See page 81.

Russell, Lord John (later Earl Russell), 1792–1878. M.P. 1813–61. A leading Whig: Prime Minister 1846–52 and 1865–6. Showed a marked interest in the idea of state education and was largely responsible for the Minutes of 1846 (together with Kay-Shuttleworth) extending the scope of government grants. Introduced the unsuccessful Education Bill of 1853. See pages 27, 36, 38, 51, 52, 53, 55, 70, 79, 80.

Shaftesbury, Earl of (formerly Lord Ashley, to 1851), 1801–85, M.P. 1826–51. Tory philanthropist and advocate of many social reforms. Largely inspired by his evangelical religious beliefs. Joined the Whigs in 1847. An active supporter of the Ragged School movement. See pages 19, 29, 30, 35, 52, 57, 58, 76, 81, 83, 86, 94, 97.

Walter, John, 1818–94. Chief proprietor of *The Times*. M.P. 1847–85. See page 70.

Whitbread, Samuel, 1758–1815. Whig M.P. 1790–1815. Introduced a Poor Law Bill in 1807 with educational clauses, but it failed to pass the House of Lords. See pages 10, 25.

Index